THE INFLUENCE OF THE ZODIAC UPON HUMAN LIFE

First Edition 1894
Eleanor Kirk

New Edition 2020
Edited by Tarl Warwick

THE INFLUENCE OF THE ZODIAC

COPYRIGHT AND DISCLAIMER

The first edition of this work is in the public domain having been written prior to 1925. This edition, with its cover art and format, is all rights reserved.

In no way may this text be construed as encouraging or condoning any harmful or illegal act. In no way may this text be construed as able to diagnose, treat, cure, or prevent any disease, injury, symptom, or condition.

THE INFLUENCE OF THE ZODIAC

FOREWORD

This fascinating little work was produced by Eleanor Kirk, a reasonably well known figure in her era who produced a fair volume of literature, some of which had a zodiacal or similar bent. This is a fairly comprehensive and authentic bit of occidental astrological lore here, although the author reminds the reader in each section (probably because some readers would only refer to the one referring to their sign!) that achieving self control and spiritual enlightenment rather nullifies fate and the star sign in favor of a fuller life.

Religious references aside, the work is very good; each sign gets its own sections on marriage compatibility, faults, positive traits, and the rearing of children for each sign; as opposed to some simplified works, it also briefly speaks about how the zodiacal signs' effect is lessened or enhanced by the movement of celestial bodies, and endorses the concept of cusp signs (of which I am, personally, being born on January 20th, therefore right at the edge of the cusp between Aquarius and Capricorn.) The work only vaguely differentiates between males and females for some purposes, and (amusingly) seems to favor the females at times- which could reflect the authors' work for womens' rights in the era.

This edition of "The Influence of the Zodiac Upon Human Life" has been carefully edited for format and content. Care has been taken to retain all original intent and meaning.

THE INFLUENCE OF THE ZODIAC

DEDICATION

To the spirit of motherhood abroad in the world, the spirit of purity and power, which should illuminate the soul and warm the heart of every true man as well as true woman, and which alone can save the race, this volume is loyally dedicated.

INFLUENCE OF THE ZODIAC UPON HUMAN LIFE

CHAPTER I

Introduction

The twelve signs of the Zodiac have always seen supposed to represent the physical framework of man. This framework is but a vessel of breath, motion, and vibration, played upon by active thought-atmospheres, waves of sound and light, and positive and negative electro-magnetic forces, in limitless activity. For ages it has been known that man's physical body was influenced by recondite or occult laws, and that to this influence could be traced the cause of the difference between individuals, between the lives of the intelligent and the ignorant, the happy and the unhappy, the good and the vicious, the useful and the useless.

The Greeks and ancient Egyptians fully recognized this truth and obeyed it conscientiously. Their children were the strongest, the handsomest, the finest in the world, and their propagation of the species, founded upon the observance of law and order, was the crowning triumph of the age. But what of today?

Our so-called advanced civilization degrades the many to exalt the few. Morality is based upon legality, and marriage,

THE INFLUENCE OF THE ZODIAC

which should be the holiest institution in the world, is often a deeper and more degraded prostitution than any other form that exists. The people who are intellectually honest and free from prejudices know that these statements are time. To every thoughtful and sympathetic man and woman the spectacle of to-day is that of quivering humanity nailed to a cross, from which rescue seems impossible. Close to our very doors we see a great multitude of men and women- flesh of our flesh, blood of our blood- living lives that are one long agony. Whence is all this error and darkness, and where is the remedy?

Ignorance is the cause and intelligence is the cure. The lust of sex and the lust of money have well nigh destroyed the world. Every child born into this world has the inalienable right of being born well. To produce unwelcome children for the sake of the gratification of a fleeting passion is a sin against God and humanity. It is time to stop. The people have been warned for many years. "The mills of the gods grind slowly, but they grind exceeding fine," and the grist bids fair to smother the world.

The scientists and philosophers of past ages, from the Greek Pythagoras to Copernicus, taught that the combined influence of the stars and planets marked the vast differentiation of animal man, and that to every human being is given in one or another direction a divine genius or talent. This genius depends upon the rhythmic harmonies of nature's universal orchestra playing upon the physical organism of man. Not to know one's genius is to be governed and tossed about by the storms of life. To be able to embrace Opportunity is to live in the native sphere from whence all harmonies proceed. The reader must ever bear in mind that there is no such thing as Fatality. These recondite laws act only upon the physical body, and are always amenable to the intelligent mind-action. The spiritual man is absolute monarch over every physical condition.

"Man is created only a little lower than the angels."

THE INFLUENCE OF THE ZODIAC

"Be ye perfect, even as your Father in heaven is perfect."

Much of the ancient knowledge in reference to harmonious companionship and the propagation of the species will be found in this volume, but, on account of the limit of the work and by the advice of wiser minds, the strictly esoteric has been only hinted at. But he who has eyes to see can read between the lines.

The inquisition of Galileo's time is not possible today. Light is gaining a victory over darkness. The true universe is being known, and dogmatism and prejudice are giving way to knowledge and tolerance. The principles found in this volume are both a science and a religion for a better and a far happier humanity.

POLARITY

True polarity is true harmony. It is perfect equilibrium, perfect poise. The result of the correct action of positive and negative forces upon an individual is health. There can be no center without the two poles- no north pole without a south pole. The power of repulsion in a positive requires the power of attraction in a negative to produce the working principle of Push and Pull, out-from and in to motion. The same principle of polarity or universal motion is found in everything. In fact, nothing can live without it. It exists in human beings, in animals, vegetables, plants, in thought, philosophy, religion, and spirit, in light and darkness, good and evil. This one great but simple principle of polarity pervades alike the natural and the spiritual worlds. Under this law, life and motion are identical. The law of reciprocity, the law of give and take, is the law of manifested universe. The law of spirit is the law of love. The union of the two is psychoplasm, or universal harmony. On the working of this principle is based the entire code of spiritual dynamics, which is Triunity.

THE INFLUENCE OF THE ZODIAC

Again, polarity is involution and evolution. There can be no evolution without involution. In every manifestation of matter or spirit there is but one great law- polarity positive, center, and negative- Triunity. What is our own Gulf Stream, flowing warm and tranquil through the heaving, restless ocean, as undisturbed and happy as a river gliding between vine-clad shores, but another illustration of the power and simplicity of polarity? The Ocean, the great resolute monarch, goes his way; the Gulf Stream, the cheery, warming, verdure-producing queen, goes her way; and so, while the great burdens of the world are carried hither and yon by our oceans, obedient to the law of reciprocity, the tranquil rivers glide through both our seas, bringing warmth and growth to those things which make the face of the earth beautiful, and so minister to the souls of men.

J. C. Street, A. B.N.

CHAPTER II

The Quickening Spirit

There has been for some time a call for a volume, simple and explanatory in style, that shall give the rudiments of what is termed Occult Science. Occult Law is simply unrevealed natural law; hidden, because until recently the world has been entirely satisfied with things as they seemed, with the external and superficial. There are many involved and expensive books dealing with this most interesting, instructive, and fascinating subject, but because they are prepared for those who have had previous instruction, they are not adapted to the needs of the thousands of people who are for the first time touched by the wing of the spirit of knowledge that now seems to be brooding and descending upon the earth. The influence of the Domains, Zodiacal Signs, Planets, and Stars has been recognized and understood by certain wise men for thousands of years, but the esoteric part of occult law has been known only to the initiated of certain nations and secret orders. The signs and wonders described by so many travelers in the East have attracted wide attention, but these phenomena have borne as small a relation to the real philosophy of occultism as the slate-writing of the modem medium bears to true Spiritualism.

The quickening spirit is here. Even the usually thoughtless and indifferent open their eyes little wider sometimes, and stop long enough in their money-grubbing and shopping to wonder what it all means. Competent teachers in mental and spiritual subjects are busy in our towns and cities, instructing great classes of students who hunger and thirst for the truths that make for peace and happiness. Dissatisfaction with old methods and theories and creeds meet us at every hand. Light has vanished upon the dark idols, and they are revealed in all their hideousness. A far-off God and a remote heaven are no

THE INFLUENCE OF THE ZODIAC

longer attractive.

The quickening spirit has breathed a thought to those who have ears to hear and hearts to feel, of the Eternal Now, and a God and a heaven in every human soul. The dogmatic absurdities of learned men are passing away. Every power of heaven and earth is friendly to a noble and courageous activity. To find out some of the causes previously ignored by the majority- even of the so-called educated and cultured- that affect for good or ill the lives of the inhabitants of the earth, has now become a vital necessity. To this end this volume is prepared, and it is hoped that it will give the student a basis upon which to build, as well as the ability to comprehend the sublime truths which every neophyte will more earnestly desire than anything that the world can offer.

An acquaintance with the Domains and Signs of the Zodiac places in the hands of every intelligent person a strong overcoming force. The first effect of this knowledge is the birth of a new charity, not only for one's neighbors but for oneself. "Receiving a new truth is adding a new sense. Eight wrongs no man."

We find that there is a reason for certain traits of character, certain passions and weaknesses "which have burdened all the conflict and hindered all the fight." The friends whom one has criticized and blamed have the same reason as ourselves for their peculiarities and unsatisfactory conduct. The next effect is the assurance that, having penetrated to the cause, it is possible to find a remedy for the conditions that have formerly ruled our lives. Many of us have laughed at what we were pleased to call the superstitions of our grandparents, especially of our grandmothers, as expressed in their devotion to the Signs of the Zodiac. Fevers turned, the sick recovered or died, children were weaned, houses bought and sold, according to some arrangement of the circle with the queer beasts and the much-

THE INFLUENCE OF THE ZODIAC

pierced man that held a place in all the almanacs of the period. Some of us have found out a few things since, and one is that it is the part of wisdom not to sneer at or condemn the things which we do not understand.

THE INFLUENCE OF THE ZODIAC

CHAPTER III

Questions and Answers

The age of Interrogation has been a long one. We have now come to the period of Response. Time will reveal every truth to posterity. Questions imply answers. Every Why holds a Because. That answers are long in coming does not prove that there are no answers. The little child demands reasons for things which his elders cannot give him. But the fact that the child is able to formulate these questions shows conclusively that the answers are not only in existence, but that he, as the seeker for this knowledge, will some time be able to answer them for himself.

That the hidden forces of the universe are more potent than those we can see and handle is a fact that the world is now beginning to accept. We have asked questions without hope of answer. Now we ask, and know that we shall receive as soon as we are willing to let go of Error and let in the Truth.

In our ignorance we have scorned the invisible and latent, and measured the universe by our five circumscribed senses. Ignorance shuts its eyes and declares itself to be right, while it is the primary source of human misery. The late tremendous progress in electrical science has been a great force in awakening the minds of the people to the realization of hidden or occult power, and it has also helped to prove the truth of the Christ statement that "there is nothing hidden which shall not be revealed." Truth is the daughter of Time. She may languish, but can never perish.

The Moon is the only planet in the heavens which has been generally credited with exerting an influence upon the Earth, and, in the minds of most people, this influence has been

THE INFLUENCE OF THE ZODIAC

confined to the tides. It is a commentary upon the intelligence of the average man and woman when the Moon, the feeblest of our luminaries, is selected as the only planet which has any relation to the Earth. These people will tell us that they know the effect of the Moon upon tides, and in the same breath will disclaim any belief in the power of other planets, which are to the Moon as the light of the Sun to a tallow candle. The light of the Moon is like the sunlight on the face of a corpse, and the power credited to it is a borrowed power, belonging of right to the Sun.

We have passed from the age of Questions and come to the age of Answers, and though we still know very little concerning the hidden or occult forces of the universe, we are learning something new every day, among which valuable information we may place the recent discovery of our previous utter ignorance of causes, and our arrogance and dogmatism in denying the powers which we were not able to test by means of our physical senses.

Truth is often too simple for us, and we do not like those who unmask our illusions; but the day has dawned, the clouds of ignorance are rolling away, and the response to the desire for knowledge is coming just as rapidly as the human soul is ready to receive it.

THE INFLUENCE OF THE ZODIAC

CHAPTER IV

Disease

Perhaps there is no term in use by meta- physicians that provokes so much ridicule from those not in sympathy with the science of mind as The Race Thought. To be told in a time of suffering, when the immediate cause is not apparent, that the unhappy conditions are attributable to the thought of disease abroad in the world is to most people a confession of weakness on the part of these philosophers and healers. But let us consider this matter a moment, and turn to the Zodiac for an illustration of this point. When the astronomers and astrologers of old placed what is called The Grand Man in the center of a circle, ranging about him the twelve signs of the Zodiac, each one, from Aries to Pisces, was made to point to the weak or vulnerable parts of the body. Look in any of the almanacs, and Taurus will be seen directing attention to the neck, Gemini to the arms, Leo to the heart, and so on. When we think that this picture has endured forages, and call to mind that our grandmothers and great-grand-mothers, although ignorant of the most vital and vitalizing principles of the cult, placed implicit confidence in the influence of these signs upon life and health, we shall be able to approximate at least to a partial comprehension of what is claimed for the Race Thought.

The ancient astrologers and scientists doubtless knew and taught that this tendency to disease had no reference to the regenerate man; that it was a condition which could influence only the person who lived exclusively in the natural and external, and in the belief of the supremacy of matter over mind. The regenerate man, or the divine human, knows that mind is the supreme master, and matter the obedient servant. So it comes to pass that the dangers pointed out by the Zodiacal signs are true as regards man in an animal condition, and absolutely false as

THE INFLUENCE OF THE ZODIAC

regards man in a spiritual state.

This explanation is vitally necessary, because the author is under an obligation to her conscience never unnecessarily to call attention to disease. Knowing that the body is what the mind makes it, and that of itself it is of no more account than a clod of dirt, it does not seem an honest thing to mention man's susceptibility to sickness without a presentation of the other and true side of the case.

The spiritual man has no master but God, and his mediator is the essential Christ, embodied in his own bosom.

THE INFLUENCE OF THE ZODIAC

CHAPTER V

Development

The threefold division of man's constitution, as illustrated in the twelve signs of the Zodiac, has long been known as triune in its nature, such as spirit, soul, and body, correspondent in their relationship of father, mother, and son, and, according to the Hermetic philosophers, objective, subjective, and passive, or sleeping- the state of inertia. The corporeal nature or animal soul of man is formed in the life of the physical body; hence man has his natural animal soul from the life of the objective natural man and of the human body, formed by man himself. The spiritual soul, or the Divine human, is the immortal individuality, which is formed by the Divine breath. Spirit, the Holy Ghost- essential soul-action from God, the life-principle of the universe in its localized and physical manifestation. There is do such thing as chance in natural and spiritual law. Every man and woman has a spiritual mission somewhere along life's journey, and it is for this mission God has created each individual.

From the glowing and the growing of the spiritual or immortal soul springs individuality. From the reason, mind, and will of the physical and corporeal man, and from the desires, appetites, and phantasies of the natural animal man, arise all the strifes in a human being.

Hence men claim "life is a warfare"; and so it is^a strife of the immortal soul to ripen out, and of the spiritual principle to illuminate the man; a strife of the rational or intellectual human will, which becomes dogmatic, often intolerant; a strife of the animal man, with his desires, ambitions, and appetites. Life is motion and action. Not to do is death. Life is kindled only by life, and, like the waters of the sea, freshens only when it ascends

THE INFLUENCE OF THE ZODIAC

to heaven. There is a natural mind and will, which are driven and tossed about by the planetary storms and solar fluids. This mind is distinguished from the intellectual reasoning principle, for there is a mind more interior than the animal mind, which is the human understanding through reason and experience. This is also quickened by the solar fluids or planetary action, for it is the genius of the natural man.

And there is a still more interior mind, the spiritual, which is absolute over all earthly or planetary conditions, which glows and continues to ripen the divine human into celestial man, whose finality is angelhood.

THE INFLUENCE OF THE ZODIAC

CHAPTER VI

A Warning

The alleged influence of some of the signs is certainly more powerful and more difficult to overcome than others. Signs that are governed by the Sun and Saturn are particularly hard, but right here let it be emphatically stated that neither Zodiacal Signs nor planets have the slightest power over the spiritualized man or woman, spirit being absolute over all matter. The stars may influence us, but God rules the stars, and when man recognizes God in himself, he can be dominated no longer by anything apart from God. It is the habit of some students to complain of their signs and planets, and in some cases rather to look down upon their neighbors who have more to contend with in this matter of overcoming natural faults. But this is unwise, because the more there is of outward conditions to work out of the greater the credit.

The student in this science is soon convinced that there is no delusion about it, and after a little practice the careful observer can calculate with almost unerring fidelity the domains of his friends and acquaintances by their general conduct and habits. The people who belong in the fiery triplicity, for instance, are as different from those who belong in the watery triplicity as fire is different from- water; the air people are entirely unlike the earth folks, and so on. When a marked difference really exists between two persons born the same day, the intelligent observer and student will immediately set about comparing the environments, always remembering that education is a most potent force in the evolution of the race. Take the hard-working washerwoman, for instance, whose life from birth has been a struggle for the bare necessities of life, and the educated and protected wife and mother, who were born under the same sign. They may not appear to have any traits in common, but if the

THE INFLUENCE OF THE ZODIAC

matter is looked into they will be found alike in fundamental characteristics. Take those again, who are on the same plane of social and intellectual life. One may show the selfishness or the quick temper that belongs to her sign, the other may appear quite thoughtless of self and as gentle as a summer breeze. The last has probably conquered the disagreeable and hindering qualities, while the former has allowed them to conquer her. If radical differences do really obtain, they can be explained by the governing planets; but these differences, comparatively speaking, are few.

The Cusp

Those who draw their first breath when one sign is giving place to another are said to be- long on the Cusp, and so partake of the characteristics of both signs. This may be an advantage or a disadvantage, according to the harmony or disharmony of the signs. Six days in a sign is said to constitute a residence, but anything less than this time endows one with some of the qualities of the preceding sign.

THE INFLUENCE OF THE ZODIAC

CHAPTER VII

Marriage Considered with Reference to Domains

If the people born in these domains Fire, Earth, Air, and Water- do really embody the qualities of their triplicities, it must be plain to the thoughtful student that the cause of many an unhappy marriage can be traced to the attempted union of uncongenial elements. This has always been ascribed as a reason, though until recently very vague notions have been held in regard to the causes of such uncongeniality.

Everybody has speculated and wondered at the quarrels and separations of the most excellent people considered individually, men and women who outside of the marital relation were the corner-stones of social and religious life. United, they were little short of demons. "It is a shame and a disgrace," has been said, "that those folks cannot get along together, and they certainly are not what they seemed to be before marriage, nor what they now appear to be when they are apart."

All can call to mind example after example of such domestic infelicity, and so alarmingly frequent is this mis-mating that long ago marriage was called "a lottery," and more lately pronounced a "failure." We have spoken of magnetic attraction and repulsion with very little idea of what we were talking about. We have witnessed the most crucial suffering of married people, for which neither wife nor husband could ascribe any adequate cause. We have observed the quick repulsions which have taken place after marriage, and which grew into unendurable hatred. We have Been the constant wife broken-hearted because of her husband's inconstancy, and faithful, noble husbands made miserable by their wives' extravagance, selfishness, and dishonor. But that there was a scientific explanation of such conditions has not been understood until lately. If the explanation

THE INFLUENCE OF THE ZODIAC

is found in the Zodiacal Domains, we must logically find in these domains the prevention of marital misery. If, for instance, one born under the head of a certain triplicity- we will take Aries, the head of the Fire- understands that it is unwise to marry one born under the head of another triplicity, and will carefully look into the reasons, a great deal of trouble will be saved. If, however, these persons have learned to control themselves and live above the influences of selfishness, anger, prejudice, envy, or whatever faults may belong to their signs, and the peculiarities of their domains, they are safe. Humanly considered, the heads of the triplicities are prone to domination, and when both husband and wife are determined to govern, harmony is an utter impossibility. Out of such a condition springs everything that is mischievous and cramping to the soul.

Persons born in the domains of Fire and Water should not marry unless there has been a thorough spiritualizing process. Water will put out fire, but fire can have little effect upon water. Marriage in these domains means usually splutter and spatter, hiss and steam. Fire and earth get along better together.

The earth is cold, and likes and needs the vitalizing and vivifying flame, and fire likes to give of itself. Still, the greatest care is necessary even here, because fire is impetuous and dominant, and we may add domineering, and expects a quick response, which the earth is not always ready to give, Those who think of uniting these domains in marriage should carefully investigate the signs under which they were born, and conscientiously examine themselves in relation to their adaptability to the new residence which they are expected to enter. The glamour of courtship is not always a safe light.

Fire and air are not always congenial elements. They have the same inspirational desires and aspirations, but they are both volatile, and sometimes the natural independence of air, as

THE INFLUENCE OF THE ZODIAC

well as its scattering qualities, prevents it from coming satisfactorily under the influences of fire. Persons from these domains make good comrades and neighbors, and are splendid workers in all reform movements. Marriage is advised between certain signs in these domains, and the information will be found in the proper place. Earth and Air are not particularly congenial elements. Earth takes Air as a matter of course, and Air is apt to feel its superiority as the breath of life.

Earth and Water mingle fairly. Mud is sometimes the result, but still it must be remembered that water molds the earth. From the blending of these elements spring all the things that minister to our necessities and make the face of the earth beautiful. Air and Water are always more or less hostile elements in the marital relation. Air people scatter, and Water people are restless. They have no more affinity for each other than a robin and a goldfish, an eagle and a whale. This, like all the rest, applies to the average undeveloped human being.

The wise reader will look into these matters and decide whether these deductions are mere theories or the truths of a great natural law. He will bring his reason to bear upon the characteristics of the domains, and by a simple process of intelligence will be able to decide upon their blending qualities. Good common sense and observation will be sufficient to prove the truth or the fallacy of the claims made for these domains, though scientific accuracy is very desirable because overwhelmingly convincing. The motto of those who find in the Zodiacal science the explanation of their domestic infelicity should be "Blessed is he who overcometh."

If one born under Aries, the head of the Fire triplicity, finds that he or she is married to one born under Cancer, the head of the Water triplicity, and through this knowledge can ac-count for the disharmony which sometimes prevails, such information should be a grand assistance instead of a matter of

THE INFLUENCE OF THE ZODIAC

discouragement, because when a cause is understood a remedy can usually be found.

With such understanding, it is possible for married people to become more to each other instead of growing farther apart, and this beautiful process can be accomplished by a careful study of self and a determination to overcome the obstacles which have prevented happiness.

THE INFLUENCE OF THE ZODIAC

THE FIRE TRIPLICITY

ARIES, LEO, SAGITTARIUS

CHAPTER VIII

ARIES: THE RAM

HEAD SIGN OF THE FIRE TRIPLICITY

March 21 to April 19

This is the head sign of the Grand Man, or macrocosm. It is a cardinal, masculine, equinoctial, and movable sign, the positive pole of tie Fire Triplicity, governing the head and face, the higher attributes being intuition and reason. The Sun enters the sign each year on or about the 21st of March, and departs from it on or about the 19th of April. The Sun on entering the sign should be given nix days before coming into full touch and action with the influence of the sign. A person born on the the date of the 21st and 27th of March would not receive the full results of the sign's individuality, as he would be born when the Sun was on the edge of the sign. This is known as the Cusp, and its nature and impulses partake of the sign the Sun has just passed through and out from, and the nature will also partake of the attributes of the sign of the Zodiac in which the Moon is located at the time of birth.

Aries is called the sign of sacrifice. People born under Aries are usually very executive, earnest, and determined. They accomplish what they resolve to do against all opposition. They are leaders, and naturally dominate those about them. They are noble, generous, magnetic, progressive, and have occult power and metaphysical tastes. They are good scholars, are bright,

THE INFLUENCE OF THE ZODIAC

genial, witty, and great talkers. They can always lead the conversation into new and interesting paths, and are never at a loss to provide entertainment. The genius of this sign is intuition, and silent electro-magnetic power by means of the hands. These people are large and true, but are apt to be children of caprice, which has a sad effect upon their destiny. They reach their highest attainment through knowledge and the regenerative love-action of the heart. They love beauty, order, harmony, and elegant surroundings. They should not be circumscribed when giving out their true work of genius. If these people are horn when the Sun is well centered in Aries, they may attain the rhythmic swing of their regenerative centers, and there arises an electro-magnetic solar fluid which is so powerful that it can be cast to a great distance; in fact, there is only one other sign so strong in this direction, and that is Aquarius.

It is almost impossible to hide anything from an Aries individual who has recognized his or her power of intuition, and for this reason those born under this sign develop quickly the gifts of the spirit. They are often excellent psychometrists, mind-readers, and spiritual comfort. They understand without words the especial trouble that is weighing upon the heart of a friend, and are frequently able to explain its cause and banish its effects. Their wills are so dominant, their sympathies so quick and kindly, and their clairvoyant power so marked, that they rarely ever fail in their work of ministering to the sorrowful. Sometimes their great regard for their friends will apparently blind them to their friends' faults, but it is doubtful if those born under this sign are ever really unaware of such weaknesses. It is a rare exception, however, when they will admit them to others, although they are not usually reticent in speaking of the failings and eccentricities of those to whom they feel no necessity of loyalty.

The Aries male will never back out of a fight. Although he will not foolishly seek one, if compelled he will go in to win,

THE INFLUENCE OF THE ZODIAC

and is always much disappointed if his side is beaten.

The Aries woman is not far behind her brother. Her friends, her favorites, are all in all, and the person who places them at a disadvantage will be dealt with in language that cannot easily be misconstrued.

The traits of Aries people often seem to contradict each other. They are not born patient, but with those they love they are sometimes patient to stupidity. They will give of their money to those who are too lazy to work for themselves, and will accept excuses and explanations with apparent credulity, although they are seldom deceived. The executive ability of those born under this sign is so marked that they occasionally come to grief from an overestimate of it. They become inflated with success, and this develops a recklessness which leads to loss and disaster, and often to nervous prostration.

The tendency with most of the Aries teachers, speakers, and writers is to give up everything to their work, and so sacrifice health and usefulness, and spoil their beautiful inspirational powers. Many fine descriptive writers, novelists, and poets are found in this sign, and many excellent teachers.

PERSONAL APPEARANCE

The Aries person is usually spare, strong, tall, quick, and sharp of sight, of oval face and swarthy complexion, with large shoulders. There are really two distinct personalities born under the sign Aries; those who are short, and those who are tall and broad-shouldered. The former are much under the influence of the Moon and the planet Mars at the time of birth, and partake somewhat of the characteristics of the signs these two planets were in. These persona are quite changeable, quick-tempered, cannot bear to be contradicted, and resent being told of their faults. If they are not permitted to do their work in their own way

THE INFLUENCE OF THE ZODIAC

they get into confusion, and very likely lose all interest in the subject. Their stubbornness is the result of the intensity of their natures, and more of an appearance than a reality. These persons are usually very fortunate in business and money-getting.

The Aries people who are tall and broad- shouldered are more silent, with a deep spiritual nature, and great occult power if they choose to develop it. They are very generous, and distinguished for their good works, but are not so fortunate in worldly affairs as those above alluded to.

COMPANIONS

They will find their best companionship and the moat genial friends with those born under Sagittarius, and nest with those in their own sign.

FAULTS

The dominant faults of persons born in this sign are selfishness, anger, and impetuosity. They are also whimsical, capricious and fickle to the last degree. They do not easily forgive their enemies, although they are rarely tempted to seek revenge for their wrongs. They will die fighting for a friend or a principle, but they will not yield a point until obliged to. These people do not like details. They are fond of planning, and are usually possessed of good taste and judgment. Women born in Aries are impatient of long seams, or the finishing-off or filling-in processes. They see how a thing looks at the start, and expect somebody else to do the work. The tendency of these people is to stifle their inspirations through externality and selfishness-inordinate selfishness, of which they are often entirely unconscious, and a propensity to talk of themselves, which earns for them oftentimes the reputation of egotists. The female destroys her best talents through jealousy, and the male through anger and quick temper. They are noted for what would be called

THE INFLUENCE OF THE ZODIAC

lost opportunities.

DISEASES

The diseases most likely to attack the people born under Aries are headache, affections of the eyes, stomach troubles, and paralysis. All these ailments and every other known to man can be entirely dominated, forever cast out, by those who realize that mind is the master and body the servant of mind.

MODE OF GROWTH

As Aries people are usually very sure that their conclusions and criticisms are unassailable, they should keep a strict count of the times when facts prove them to be wrong. They will find themselves frequently mistaken. They should put a bridle on their tongues, and learn to join in a conversation in a temperate manner, and not to assume the whole responsibility of it. They should learn to avoid repetition, and to understand that a strong statement once made is always weakened by a second one. They should practice silence, and spend some time each day alone. Any process that will restrain the action of the tongue and the determination to govern everybody and everything will be found wholesome and legitimate. Their natural impetuosity often leads them into serious blunders, and these complications are entirely unnecessary, because, if those born under this sign will be led by their own uninfluenced, unmeddled-with intuitions, they will see and do the right. They should come to their conclusions when alone, and learn to place a proper value on the genius of their sign. These people need no stimulants, and they should eat plain, nourishing food with regularity. They should not surrender themselves, body and soul, to their friends and their pursuits, but learn to listen, wait, and expect the higher revelations of life and truth, which are theirs to command.

THE INFLUENCE OF THE ZODIAC

MARRIAGES

The most harmonious domestic life is found when an Aries and a Sagittarius person are united. The offspring will he strong physically, bright intellectually, and of a superior nature. The marriage of an Aries person with one in the same sign is usually harmonious, but the children are not so strong physically, and will not show so much talent. When united with those born under other signs, the domestic life will be at best only a compromise, with few and perhaps no children.

These conditions depend much upon whether the contracting parties are on the same plane of material and social life.

GOVERNMENT OF CHILDREN

The children born under this sign should not be driven, teased, or in any way hurt or abused. They can be readily controlled if they are allowed to do their little tasks in their own way. When they are wrong or angry, kindly ask permission to help them; if they refuse, do not persist, and do not scold, but await opportunity; when it offers, kindly reason with them. Love is the conqueror of all born under this sign. They should be kept as free from excitement as possible. Both young and old require much sleep, and they should occupy large rooms with plenty of fresh air. The natural individuality of these children should be recognized, and very tactfully dealt with. Great discretion is necessary in the use of praise or commendation. They require the stimulus of ready appreciation, but it should never be given by comparison with others to the disadvantage of the latter. They are apt to think too much and talk too much of themselves, and so it is always judicious to hold up other children as examples in well-doing.

THE INFLUENCE OF THE ZODIAC

An Aries child should be early taught to consult the comfort and happiness of others, and never to expect the head places. Yet, they should not be discouraged or hindered in any ambition, save the one which exalts self. They can be developed into loyal, willing servers, and they will soon understand the nature of their special gifts and know bow to use them. The work of education should commence in babyhood, for they are very quick to perceive any weakness in those who have the care of them, and when once their small hands grasp the reins of power it is not an easy matter to regain possession.

The governing planets are Mars and Neptune, and the gems are amethyst-Brazilian, and diamond. The astral colors are white and rose pink.

THE INFLUENCE OF THE ZODIAC

CHAPTER IX

LEO THE LION

MIDDLE SIGN OF THE FIRE TRIPLICITY

July 22 to August 22

This is the heart of the Grand Man or Macrocosm. It is a masculine, commanding, fixed, choleric, fiery, changeable, northern sign of the Zodiac, the middle point of the magnet of the Fire Triplicity. It governs the heart and blood of life, the higher attributes being belief and self-control. The Sun enters the sign Leo on or about the 22nd of July each year, and departs from the sign on or about the 22nd of August. It takes six days for the Sun to come into full touch and action with the sign. Therefore, a person born between the dates of the 22nd and the 28th of July would not receive the full central results of the sign's individuality, as this person would be born on the edge of the Zodiac, which is known as the Cusp. Its impulses partake of the sign the Sun has just passed through and out from. The native thus born will partake much of the attributes of the sign of the Zodiac, wherein the Moon is located at the time of birth.

The people born under this sign are kind-hearted, generous, sympathetic, and magnetic. They make good nurses when in full sympathy with the patient. They are emotional, very intuitive, and are generally able by means of this power to escape the consequences of their actions. Leo people are fine conversationalists, excelling in repartee, and are the best of story-tellers. They always make a point, and always see the point. When the true individuality of Leo holds sway, these people have a noble ideal, with a loyal love, confident, pure, and abundant. Having minds of the practical, philosophical, and spiritual combined- a triunity- they radiate a luminous substance,

THE INFLUENCE OF THE ZODIAC

which makes them a most powerful people for good, with a marked ability to inspire others.

Under such conditions they have the most remarkable power in molding public opinion, and in swaying great audiences. In fact, the truly awakened Leo men and women are invincible if they will learn the pathway of silence. Leo people have a great love for their own, and will not yield to advice or dictation in the management of their children. Leo women who have been looked upon as angels in the neighborhood will sometimes show an astonishing ferocity if their children are hurt or reproved. A fault found with them, a complaint made by a teacher or a friend, will arouse these mothers to the highest pitch of passionate excitement. The motto of the Leo woman is "Love me, love my dog." The natural intuition of these people is very great, and this talent is sometimes so constantly exercised that it leads to deep-seated aversion and prejudice.

They have been right in their estimates of people six times out of ten, therefore they must be right ten times out of ten. Argument is of no use under such conditions. In fact, it is well to let the Leo person enjoy his opinions without interference. The balance of happiness for the rest of the family is usually to be found in that method. Those born under this sign are in some respects near of kin to those who come under the head of the same triplicity. They would rather plan than work, and they are by no means fond of details. They are sometimes very lazy, and, like the cat, are fond of basking in the sun and dozing in the chimney corner. They are fond of all creature and home comforts. The men usually know where the best markets are to be found, and have a real genius in catering for the table. The women have the same talent in selecting, and among them are found our most inspirational cooks.

THE INFLUENCE OF THE ZODIAC

PERSONAL APPEARANCE

Usually persons born under this sign have a strong wiry body, not over tall, but well proportioned, broad shoulders, round head, with light or ruddy complexions, strong, deep voice, and large eyes, and are often under a peculiar spiritual influx.

COMPANIONS

Companionships and true genial friends for Leo people will usually be found first among Sagittarius people, next among those born under Libra, or under Aries.

FAULTS

The faults of these people are most marked. Many of them are cunning, tricky, natural prevaricators, and chronic borrowers. They are hot-headed, impetuous, fiery, and passionate. They are easily attracted by the opposite sex, and are not usually distinguished for constancy. They take quick prejudices, but are sometimes more correct in their estimate of people than their cooler-headed and more passive neighbors. There are occasional liars to be found in this sign, and like the cat some of them will appropriate that which is not given them. Leo is the only sign in the Zodiac that is governed by the Sun. and to this solar influence is ascribed the passion and impetuosity of those who come under it. These faults are some- what modified in Leo women, proving the truth of what has been previously stated, that training and environment have their influence upon the mighty planetary forces. Our girls are more sheltered and carefully educated than our boys; they cannot give rein to their natural impulses, and so learn to dominate them. But a Leo woman who has not thus controlled herself will be apt to go even farther in duplicity and appetite than a Leo man. When these faults are overcome, there is no better, stronger, or more helpful

THE INFLUENCE OF THE ZODIAC

person among all the signs of the Zodiac.

DISEASES

The diseases to which Leo people are liable arise from weakness of lungs, heart trouble3, violent fevers, back and kidney troubles, which any long-continued despondency will greatly increase. All these ailments and every other known to man can be entirely dominated, forever cast out, by those who realize that mind is the master and body the servant of mind.

MODE OF GROWTH

The spiritual evolution of the Leo character is by cool and passive contemplation and silence. They should ever bear in mind that their governing planet is the Sun, and that true growth can be attained only by a combination of heat and cold, light and shadow. Their best discipline seems to come from suffering, loss, and sickness, through which they learn the futility of deception and passion. Every Leo individual should be sure to set apart some moments each day for silence and repose; also periods of absolute solitude. Only in this way can true polarity be obtained.

The greatest pains should be taken by those born under this sign to discriminate between natural intuition, which is theirs to a remarkable degree, and the abuse of this native genius, which degenerates into a mean and hurtful prejudice. They should try to see that this latter trait of character is a positive hindrance to their own growth, because hurtful to others. They also need to exercise themselves more in regard to the comfort and happiness of others, and less in regard to their own. The selfishness of this sign must be overcome before there can be any true progress. Leo people should often take a careful inventory of their own faults and weaknesses, and in this way learn charity for others.

THE INFLUENCE OF THE ZODIAC

MARRIAGES

In the selection of husband or wife the greatest care. should be taken; otherwise long-continued troubles will be the result. A union with a person born in Sagittarius or in Aries is likely to be most happy and to produce the strongest offspring. The reader must remember that usually the happiest results arise in marriage where social and intellectual equality exists.

GOVERNMENT OF CHILDREN

Children who are born when the Sun is well centered in Leo should be most carefully guarded, on account of having fine sensitive natures, with a strong emotional impulse to imitate others. They are very apt to lack individuality. Special instruction should be given to teach self-control in all animal and sex functions. Without a strong hand and proper education, these children are very apt to partake of many vices and evils which lead to paralysis, consumption, or insanity. A great responsibility rests upon parents and guardians who have the charge of these younger people. Leo children are quick to observe any duplicity or inconsistency on the part of those around them, and will meet it all with corresponding hypocrisy and a deep cunning. They are exceedingly imitative, and must therefore be taught independence of character. They not only imitate the actions and the faults of others, but they have a great power in imitating voices and gestures. They must never be aroused to combat, but a constant endeavor must be made to raise them above the common level of humanity. Such training requires line upon line, and precept upon precept. If parents could be made to understand the grand possibilities of the regenerate Leo character, they would not spare themselves in this educatory work. The minds of these sensitive and talented children should be kept busy with simple, wholesome, and amusing tasks.

THE INFLUENCE OF THE ZODIAC

There can be no harmonious development of a child born under this fiery and impulsive sign without constant and varied amusement, Just as a young lion can be brought into subjection by steadfast love and unvarying kindness, so can the little human lion be tamed and developed into all goodness. He must be constantly under observation, but must not know it. If he is conscious of being watched, he will immediately commence to deceive and prevaricate. These little ones should never be pushed one side. They should be the constant companions of judicious parents or guardians. Parents must be careful not to transgress the rules they have made for these little ones. The true nature of the higher individuality of Leo is law and order; but many Leo people go through life from the cradle to the grave without being appreciated, or even understood.

This sign is governed by the Sun, and the gems are ruby and diamond. The astral colors are red and green.

THE INFLUENCE OF THE ZODIAC

CHAPTER X

SAGITTARIUS THE ARCHER

LAST SIGN OF THE FIRE TRIPLICITY

November 22 to December 21

This sign governs the thighs of the Grand Man, or Macrocosm. It is a masculine, diurnal, eastern, double-bodied, speaking, choleric, dual, fortunate sign of the Zodiac, the negative pole of the Fire Triplicity, governing the thighs, hips, and the motor nerve system. The higher attributes are love and introspection. The Sun enters the sign Sagittarius on or about the 22nd of November, and departs from it on or about the 21st of December of each year. The Sun, just entering the sign, should be given six days before coming into full touch and action with the influence of the sign. Therefore a person born between the dates of the 22nd and 28th of November would not receive the full central results of the sign's individuality, as he would be born when the Sun was on the edge of the sign. This is known as the Cusp, and its nature and impulses partake of the sign the Sun has just passed through and out from, and the native will also partake of the attributes of the sign of the Zodiac in which the Moon is located at the time of birth. The people born under this sign usually aim well and hit the mark in all matters. Because of this characteristic they are prophetic, and can tell the outcome of almost any enterprise from its inception. They rarely make mistakes when they follow their own inspirations, but are sure to be led astray if they rely upon the advice of others. Sagittarius people are born busy, and keep busy under all circumstances. They are distinguished for minding their own business and keeping their own secrets. They do not trouble their neighbors affairs, but are exceedingly active in their own. They always want to finish one thing before they begin another, and are as

THE INFLUENCE OF THE ZODIAC

remarkable for their carefulness in detail as are the Aries people for carelessness or inability. These people are enterprising, progressive, and far-seeing, always courageous in an emergency, but frequently timid and afraid when there is no need for action or quick thought. An emergency is an inspiration. They are neat and orderly, and very careful in money matters, saving, but not penurious. It is seldom that you find a Sagittarius man or woman without money. Their talents are varied, and they can earn a dollar while others are deploring the need of one.

The women are fine housekeepers, excellent wives, and usually judicious mothers. They have a great love for children and animals. This is also a musical sign, and an occult sign, as those under its influence naturally turn to the spiritual side of life and make the most useful teachers. These people see things entirely different from the rest of humanity. Belonging to the realm of prophecy, they are also naturally clairvoyant and clairaudient. They hear words and see visions that the world knows not of. Their minds reach out far beyond the present, and so it comes to pass that a Sagittarius person is often accused of fabrication. These people always mean to tell the truth, All Sagittarius people are of one thought and one idea at a time. More than one thing on their hands at the same time distresses them. They are very decided in everything they do. They frequently jump at conclusions before properly weighing by calm reason the full consequences and difficulties, but being very hopeful, they often overcome very great obstacles. They are quick to foresee events, even to small things; are very apt to speak out their own conclusions and feel sure they are right, and hence often make enemies, for people do not usually wish to be told the truth in plain words. Almost all of these people are very blunt and outspoken for what they feel is true, but right and truth wrong no man. There is a power about them that makes their words strike home, even though the persona addressed are unwilling to admit their correctness. When these words are entirely free from anger and resentment, they compel

THE INFLUENCE OF THE ZODIAC

attention and often reformation; but the impetuosity of those born under this sign is very apt to dim or spoil the effect of the truth.

Sagittarius people are very apt to be misunderstood. They see so clearly, think so quickly, and because of this natural intuition are so sure of being correct, that they very often strike squarely against the opinions and prejudices of those about them. This leads to discussion, unrest, and perhaps serious quarrels. They cannot bear to see suffering. The first impulse is to relieve it, and they spare neither time, money, nor strength in this work. This labor is always one of the heart, but strange to say it is usually repaid with ingratitude. Their generosity and goodness are constantly taken advantage of. This is the cause of great sorrow and bitterness, and wounds so deeply as to almost paralyze all effort and all desire to be of use.

PERSONAL APPEARANCE

These people have very expressive eyes, and are fine looking; they have jovial dispositions, and are fearless and daring when doing duty, or living upon a principle. The silent ones are usually quite tall and slender. The active ones are more robust and are very graceful, being swift in all their movements.

COMPANIONS

These people will find their best friends among Aries, Sagittarius, Aquarius, and Libra people.

FAULTS

People born in this sign have a tendency to fly all to pieces over a small matter, are quick to anger, but quickly over it, combative, and determined to have their own way. As enemies Sagittarius people go to extremes. They may forgive, and treat

THE INFLUENCE OF THE ZODIAC

the one who has injured them with kindness, but they do not forget. They are unreasonable in their desire to help those they love, and are zealous and over-sanguine in whatever they undertake. They are unwilling to wait for proper times and sea- sons, and desire to rush through every piece of work as soon as it presents itself. An unfinished task is an intolerable affliction; therefore Sagittarius people, especially the women, are likely to sacrifice health and good nature in their determination to finish what they commence.

This alertness and incessant industry frequently causes trouble in the family. Those born under less active signs cannot see how it is possible for one to be forever busy. Sometimes these workers are very fond of their achievements and are exceedingly unhappy and disappointed if their labors are not properly appreciated. The Sagittarius person who has had no training in governing the faults of his sign, always aims in his anger at the vulnerable spot of his enemy and is reasonably sure to hit it. Such a one when angered is very cruel. These people expect too much of others. They are quick to observe, to plan and to do, and they make small allowance for those who are less gifted in such practical respects. Until they have learned self-control they are apt to be very exacting and domineering.

DISEASES

The diseases most likely to attack these people are weakness of the lungs, rheumatism, and stomach troubles.

All these ailments and every other known to man can he entirely dominated forever cast out by those who realize that mind is the master and body the servant of mind.

THE INFLUENCE OF THE ZODIAC

MODE OF GROWTH

As the lot of those born under this sign is to be misunderstood, it is best for them to have very few confidential friends. They should cultivate calmness and repose, and think well and in silence before deciding any important question. They should not be governed by impulse in any charitable work. They should strive to find their reward for service in the unselfish motive which prompted it, and expect neither gratitude nor appreciation from any source but their own consciences. This is a hard battle, but blessed indeed are those who conquer. The bluntness of Sagittarius people is the cause of much unnecessary suffering to others, and they must not excuse themselves because of the truth of their words. They should learn to be gentle in speech, and to give out the truth with discrimination. They should teach themselves not only to forgive but to forget ingratitude. Ingratitude is often returned for unselfish service, but they should not be disheartened. They should do good to all and pass on, realizing that God understands.

MARRIAGE

As has been stated, a harmonious domestic life will be obtained by the union of a Sagittarius and an Aries person. The offspring will be intellectually bright, of marked genius, and usually robust. Sagittarius and Aquarius people have been known to unite well in marriage, though trouble often comes through the coldness and lack of responsiveness of the Aquarius mate. The union of Sagittarius and Sagittarius is usually harmonious; the offspring will be bright and quick, but not quite so strong as the offspring of Aries and Sagittarius.

These people should be very careful in marrying, as serious troubles are apt to occur from uncongenial unions. They despise all licentiousness, being naturally pure in thought and

THE INFLUENCE OF THE ZODIAC

intention. Their demand for purity and individuality in married life often causes great in- harmony. These people are all very strong and loyal in their love relations, but when they are deceived or ill-treated it is apt to embitter their future happiness. The women become silent and hopeless, while the men are likely to indulge in drink or reckless despondency. A Sagittarius woman is apt to avenge a proffered insult with a blow. The Archer never wastes the ammunition of words upon such cases.

It should be remembered that the happiest unions result when the contracting parties are on the same plane of intellectual and social life.

GOVERNMENT OF CHILDREN

Children born under this sign must be trusted and made companions of. They cannot be easily deceived, because they know from within. It is easier by far to conquer a city than to restore to them a confidence when once it has been broken. These children should be kept active by means of simple pursuits through most of the waking hours, and as far as possible should be allowed to choose their occupations. They are apt to be almost morbidly sensitive, and their feelings are very easily hurt. They require a constant expression of love from those who have the care of them and whom they love. They are grateful little creatures, and will perform any service to win a loving caress or a word of praise.

These children must be kept close to the heart, or they grow unmanageable through their disappointment. They belong to the very inmost soul of things, and coldness and indifference chill and destroy them. These little ones are very fond of other children, and this love should be fostered by parents and guardians. They early show that they are not merely attracted by personality, for the lame, the halt, and the blind are always the ones who are singled out for especial attention.

THE INFLUENCE OF THE ZODIAC

A colored child or a child with a dirty face is not obnoxious to the average Sagittarius little one. The faces and hands can be washed, and this is what the young Archer usually proceeds to do. It is a great mistake for parents to interfere with this universal love and friendliness, for it is a rare and much-needed element in a world chiefly noted for harsh criticisms and devotion to personality.

The governing planet is Jupiter, and the gems are carbuncle, diamond, and turquoise. The astral colors are gold, red, and green.

THE AIR TRIPLICITY

GEMINI, LIBRA, AQUARIUS

CHAPTER XI

GEMINI THE TWINS

HEAD SIGN OF THE AIR TEIPLICITY

May 20 to June 21

This sign governs the shoulders, arms, and hands of the Grand Man. or Macrocosm. It is a changeable, masculine, double- bodied, common, commanding sign, the positive pole of the Air Triplicity. The higher attributes are reason and sensation. The Sun enters the sign Gemini each near on or about the 20th of May, and departs from the sign on or about the 21st of June. The Sun on entering the sign should be given six days before coming into full touch and action with the influence of the sign. A person born between the dates of the 20th and 27th of May would not receive the full central results of the sign's individuality as he would be born when the Sun was on the edge of the sign. This is known as the Cusp, and its nature and impulses partake of the sign the Sun has just passed through and out from, and the native will also partake of the attributes of the sign of the Zodiac in which the Moon is located at the time of birth.

Many Gemini persons may be said to be double. One trait of character seems to contradict another trait- in other words, they have a dual nature in active operation. They want to travel, and they want to stay at home. They wish to study, and they wish to play. They are happy and unhappy, satisfied and dissatisfied at the same time. They are in love and not in love;

THE INFLUENCE OF THE ZODIAC

warm and cold in one breath. The Gemini people do not fly quite as high as the other denizens of the Air Triplicity, because the twins are not always agreed upon the destination. This contradiction causes a state of nervousness which is very hard to overcome. Gemini people are extremely affectionate and generous, very courteous and kind to all. They are proud of birth, and have a great deal of family pride. They are not a selfish or a penurious people. They are thoughtful of the poor, and very sympathetic with the suffering. They are fond of the arts and sciences, are great readers and good talkers, and very quick to see the point of a story or joke. These people are not usually successful wage -earners, and frequently give away as fast as they can earn.

They have very strong religious natures, and are often found among church members. A creed is of great importance to their happiness, and yet they rarely place implicit confidence in any theological system, though they will stoutly defend the one they have appeared to espouse. Gemini people have a great respect for religious teachers, and are sometimes very timid and apprehensive about thinking for themselves. This is attributable to the necessity they feel for something to lean upon, and the small opinion they have of their own ability to decide questions of moment, There are no more affectionate, unselfish, and self-sacrificing people in all the twelve signs of the Zodiac than those who come under Gemini. Gemini people are often very executive with their hands, and can cut and plan, and see into a device or pattern, and. if not interfered with, will bring the work to beautiful completion. But they are not able to tell beforehand how they are going to do it. Explanations and arguments are impossible to the average Gemini person- in fact, to most of the Air people. Gemini women are especially fond of color, and of flowers, and of everything beautiful in nature and art.

The finest efforts of the writers and poets that come under this sign are reached by inspiration and not by analysis or

THE INFLUENCE OF THE ZODIAC

previous intellectual preparation. Both Emerson and Margaret Fuller Ossoli were born under Gemini, and are splendid illustrations of the true Gemini genius.

PERSONAL APPEARANCE

Those born under this sign are usually well formed, of dark hair and bright complexion, with a sharp quick eye, usually of hazel color.

COMPANIONS

For true friends and companionship, Gemini individuals will find the best results with calm, quiet, and reserved people, first those born under Aquarius and those from Virgo.

FAULTS

The faults of persons born under this sign are a scattering of force and great unrest. They are natural complainers and growth and imagine evil. They are never still, though a responsibility or a duty will settle these people with as much alacrity as those born under other signs. They crave knowledge, but are exceedingly impatient of methods. These are the people who most deceive themselves. Some of the best public speakers and lecturers are born under this sign, but they have attained eminence only by a great struggle for continuity, and by honesty with themselves. They have two distinct natures, which are the Castor and Pollux of Greek mythology, and are continually crucifying each other. These people are very anxious and expectant, and often so restless and nervous that they destroy their health. They are liable to go to the extreme in every thing they do; always hunting for occupation and anxious to go, and to do something, they know not what, and are filled with a dissatisfaction which nothing can explain. They are given to regrets, are very suspicious, and very untruthful. The Gemini

THE INFLUENCE OF THE ZODIAC

person who has not come into a knowledge of spiritual truths is exceedingly apt to think entirely of the personality of those he is associated with. If the external appearance is pleasing, and grace and beauty charm the eye, there is nothing more to be desired. Many Gemini women come to grief by their superficial judgment in such matters. As they are very affectionate and demonstrative, they suffer jealousy from the neglect and indifference of those they have mistakenly elevated to places they were never intended to occupy.

DISEASES

The diseases from which these people are likely to suffer are throat and lung troubles, nervous diseases, and nervous prostration. Children, as well as grown persons, under this sign are often troubled with stomach worms and eczema. These maladies and every other known to man, can be entirely dominated, forever cast out, by those who realize that mind is the master and body the servant of mind.

MODE OF GROWTH

The only rest and repose for Gemini people will be found in metaphysical study and practice, and spiritual revealment, They must learn patience and silence, keep the conversation free from personality, remembering that heaven is within the temple of the human breast, and not outside of it. They must learn continuity and consistency, and they should never permit themselves to do the acts they have condemned in others. They should firmly resolve never to complain or murmur, as this habit increases with practice to an awful extent, making the elderly people born under this sign very disagreeable in the family. Silence and passive reason, with introspection, are the true inner pathways of spiritual illumination. Gemini people should learn to keep their feet and hands still. The restlessness of these members is a true symptom of the restlessness of the spirit,

THE INFLUENCE OF THE ZODIAC

and the determination to conquer a physical expression very quickly has its influence upon the subjective mind. They should strive for unity of purpose, thus overcoming the propensity of Castor and Pollux to pull in opposite directions. They should realize the glaring faults of a nature that dislikes to-day the things that were coveted yesterday. They should determine to free themselves forever from their tendency to sit in judgment upon their fellow-creatures.

MARRIAGE

A union with a person born in Aquarius or Virgo is likely to be most happy. The offspring will then be strong and bright. When united with an Aquarius person, children are usually very bright and quick of intellect, but when united with almost any other sign, life, as far as domestic relations are concerned, is not likely to be one of satisfaction. These conditions depend much upon whether the contracting parties are on the same plane of material and social life.

GOVERNMENT OF CHILDREN

Children born in this sign should be associated with persons who are quiet, calm, and restful. They are often thrown into fits, and women into hysterics, by undue excitement and nervous disturbances. The best training for both young and old born under this sign is to learn to talk slowly and cultivate calmness. These children often become ill from no apparent cause. Such condition is usually caused by worms and by too rapid eating. They should be carefully guarded against looking for evil, as this soon grows into vague imaginings of evil and error everywhere. This tendency is seldom eradicated in later years, producing the most unhappy results in an old age full of suspicion and distrust. The governing planet is Mercury, and the gems are beryl, aquamarine, and dark-blue stones. The astral colors are red, blue, and white.

THE INFLUENCE OF THE ZODIAC

CHAPTER XII

LIBRA, THE SCALES

MIDDLE SIGN OF THE AIR TRIPLICITY

September 23 to October 23

This sign governs the loins and reins of the Grand Man, or Macrocosm. It is a cardinal, sanguine, diurnal, movable, airy, equinoctial, masculine sign of the Zodiac. This is the great equatorial line of human progression; the higher attributes are perception and inspiration. The Sun enters the sign each year on or about the 23rd of September, and departs from it on or about the 23rd of October. The Sun on entering a sign should be given six days before coming into full touch and action with the influence of the sign. A person born between the dates of the 23rd and 29th of September would not receive the full results of the sign's individuality, as he would be born when the Sun was on the edge of the sign. This is known as the Cusp, and its nature and impulses partake of the sign the Sun has just passed through and out from, and the native will also partake of the attributes of the sign of the Zodiac in which the Moon is located at the time of birth.

People born under this sign are energetic, ambitions, generous, and inspired. The men and women are said to differ even more than Leo men and women, and probably from the same reason. The Libra men having had to seek their own way, and to find their own companions and occupations, early learn to tune their inspirations and their clairvoyant ability to financial account, and so become stock brokers and sometimes gamblers. The scales of Libra tip very easily, and too often one scale touches bottom with a dead weight, while the other swings aloft unused and empty. Libra men are very fascinating, and they are

THE INFLUENCE OF THE ZODIAC

as reckless in following out the gratification of their desires as they are in gambling games and speculations. This pursuit is not so much sensual as sensuous, and is more of an eagerness for new objects of attraction than an impulse of passion. "When overtaken by disaster, they recover quickly and go to work again with redoubled vigor. Their feet never touch the earth in their calculations and intrigues. They are full of hope and enthusiasm, and crash after crash produces no effect. The Libra women who have not had the masculine liberty are not so reckless as their brothers. They are apt to be careless about money matters, and this is often due to their extreme aversion to the financial part of any transaction. They detest to be mixed up with money matters. They are not intentionally dishonest, for they always expect to be able to pay their debts, and often borrow with the noblest intentions, but if anything occurs to thwart their calculations- and ten to one it does- they expect the person borrowed from to he as magnanimous in forgiving the debt an they would be in paying it if they had the money. And yet these people, both men and women, have a keen and beautiful sense of justice; they are also exceedingly intuitive and mediumistic. When spiritualized, the scales hang evenly balanced, and the work that can be accomplished for humanity by the Libra people cannot be overestimated. Among them are poets, writers, and musicians. They soar high because the most rarefied air is their native element. They will give away the largest half of anything they possess, and never expect an equivalent. They are timid and apprehensive of disaster to their children and friends, and cause much nervous anxiety to their families and others.

Those born under this sign, especially the women, are so sensitive to harmony or disharmony that they can tell as soon as they enter a house what the prevailing conditions are. This sometimes makes them appear sad, indifferent, or disturbed, and they are considered very disagreeable and inconsistent. Their high spirits are subdued, and a shadow falls upon all who are in their company. As it is not usually safe or proper to explain the

THE INFLUENCE OF THE ZODIAC

reason of the cloud, the victims are obliged to suffer and be silent. This tendency to feel every change in those about them, and to read secret thoughts is a constant menace to the best development. It keeps the individual harassed by anxieties which cannot be relieved or spoken of. In this way the sympathies are kept in constant action and without subserving any good purpose. When this psychic power is dominated by the will, and made to mind its own business, and keep out of other people's affairs, it is a wonderful force, but, used on a lower plane, is a source of unrest and misery.

Libra women are very kind and amiable, and are averse to any cruelty and bloodshed. The women and children dislike to know that even a chicken must be killed. They are very neat, and dislike any hard and dirty work. The other type of Libra people is to he found more among the males who have broad, round foreheads, and are cunning and quick speculators, having wonderful perceptive faculties. These will usually be found in the stock markets, where they are very fortunate. These men are apt to be very inconstant. Libra people are psychic collectors of thought, having the ability to acquire the occult laws of nature. Possessing the power of perception of spiritual knowledge, they can reach the highest goal of human attainment by bringing their powers to a center within the bosom. Those who recognize the dawning of the life regenerate, can acquire the divine and hidden mysteries of the ages.

PERSONAL APPEARANCE

In physical appearance these people are usually tall, slender, and well formed, with oval face, quick enunciation, sometime shrill voice, and beautiful eyes.

THE INFLUENCE OF THE ZODIAC

COMPANIONS

The highest companionship and most congenial friends will be found among Fire people; best, with those born under their own sign; and, third, with those born in Aquarius.

FAULTS

Libra people are apt to take things from a material, literal standpoint, and though their fine interior nature will often show them the true soul-side of the question, yet they often prefer and accept the conclusions of human logic. They are very impatient, and this causes them to lose much of their vital force, often bringing pains across the small of the back, When they grow out of the lower desires, they make the most devoted and loving companions and parents.

These people are prodigal of their strength and talents, and scatter their forces in all directions. They feel it their imperative duty to help everybody, and seem to be utterly unaware of the fact that the ability to assist others is born of the power to govern self. It is exceedingly difficult for a Libra person to appreciate this truth. These are the people who are easily confused and confounded by the arguments of others, and who seem panic-stricken when lost in a crowd or compelled to cross busy streets. They are usually careless of their belongings, and are apt to drop and lose things. These are they who borrow books and do not always return them, and who are impatient of criticism on all subjects of omission or commission. They have an unbounded desire for the approbation of others, and are foolishly wounded by trifles. They often seem more unreasonable and inconsistent than they really are, because of the working of the sixth sense- intuition- which constantly acquaints them with the thoughts and feelings, states and conditions, of those about them.

THE INFLUENCE OF THE ZODIAC

Libra people are apt to espouse a new cause too readily, and often get into trouble through their enthusiasm, which seems never to diminish from the cradle to the grave. They are impatient of methods, and despise necessary routine. When angered, which is seldom, they leave nothing unsaid. The effect is like a cyclone, which leaves the air disturbed and cloudy for days afterward.

DISEASES

The diseases of those born under this sign are nervous prostration, and peculiar stomach troubles, which are brought about by excessive worry and impatience, and happen only when the Libra people live on the lower animal plane. All these ailments, and every other known to man, can be entirely dominated, forever cast out, by those who realize that mind is master, and the body the servant of mind.

MODE OF GROWTH

Libra people should strive for habits of order even in small things, and should take to heart the truth that nothing is insignificant which promotes the peace and pleasure of others. They should curb their desire for praise and appreciation, and never do a kind action for the credit to be derived from it. They should labor to overcome the habit of exaggeration, which, from an over-enthusiasm, is very marked in this sign, and watch every thought that wells up from the heart and every word that passes the lips.

Each and every individual born under this sign should have a retiring place, or sanctuary, which should really be a holy place. In this way they will find peaceful repose, the illumination of the spirit, and inspiration through divine truth will flow in like a fountain of light. They should make a careful study and exercise of psychic perception, with a full knowledge of the

THE INFLUENCE OF THE ZODIAC

difference between intuition, outside perception, and psychic understanding. When this knowledge is once attained, these people can be perfect encyclopedias of information. The exceptions are those engulfed in the lower animal appetites. When Libra people go to extremes, they are very dishonest indeed. Just so long as they follow their own intuitions they will rarely be deceived. When any important subject is involved, they should come to conclusions when entirely alone, as they are more or less subject to the positive mind action of others.

The influx of the word of the spirit comes by perception and harmonious emotion. To cultivate the divine inward breath is most beneficial to all Libra people. Learn patience, silence, and repose, Libra, and your possibilities are great.

MARRIAGE

When a Libra and a Sagittarius person are united, the children will be very talented. Children of Libra and Aquarius will be stronger physically, and will possess a keen intellect. One born under Libra should never unite with one born under Pisces. And strange as it may appear, a Pisces person will usually choose from Libra in marriage. A Pisces person continually demands reasons and full explanations of actions and motives. A Libra person can seldom give reasons. These people can make but few explanations, hence much misunderstanding is the result, ending perhaps in the divorce court. A Libra person should never unite (with exceedingly few exceptions) with a person born under Virgo, as these people are so critical in their judgments, and especially so if intellectually cultivated. Aries and Libra people often make the closest friends. Their greatest care should he exercised in any and all companionship for those born under this sign.

THE INFLUENCE OF THE ZODIAC

GOVERNMENT OF CHILDREN

Very few people can understand Libra children. They are exceedingly true and good, or very unreliable, quick-tempered, and prone to evil. They are very susceptible to psychological influences, and frequently say and do things they themselves cannot account for, and which cause great anxiety to parents and guardians. They require a special and positive drill that they may become acquainted with the laws of nature from all her standpoints. They should fully comprehend the laws of generation when young, and not be deceived by prudish and conventional training. As they are quite apt to have a high temper, they should be lovingly reasoned with after the temper has passed away. They are quick to perceive the truth in anything, and will make determined efforts to improve. These little folks have usually a natural genius for invention and originality of thought and design, having a marked mechanical ability over all the other signs. Teachers should see to it that these young minds are opened and illuminated through their own natural bent of genius and originality of producing things. They should always be permitted to have their own way when not entirely wrong. To circumscribe a Libra child is to destroy its genius. These children often see, hear, and feel things that those about them are utterly unconscious of and not infrequently learn to deceive, because their explanations are doubted or made fun of.

The governing planet is Venus, and the gems are diamond and opal. The astral colors are black, crimson, and light blue.

THE INFLUENCE OF THE ZODIAC

CHAPTER XIII

AQUARIUS, THE WATER BEARER

LAST SIGN OF THE AIR TRIPLICITY

January 20 to February 19

This sign governs the legs of the Grand Man, or Macrocosm. It is an aerial, sanguine, masculine, western, fixed, human, rational, speaking, obeying sign, the negative pole of the Air Triplicity. In its spiritual duality it is the sign of the Divine Sophia, the attributes being soul, memory, and diffusive knowledge. It governs the physical memory. The Sun enters the sign each year on or about the 20th of January and departs from it on or about the 19th of February. The Sun on entering the sign should be given six days before coming into full touch and action with the influence of the sign. A person born between the dates of the 20th and 26th of January would not receive the full central results of the sign's individuality. as he would be born when the Sun was on the edge of the sign. This is known as the Cusp, and its nature and impulses partake of the sign the Sun has just passed through and out from, and the native will also partake of the attributes of the sign of the Zodiac in which the Sun is located at the time of birth.

People born under this sign are said to be the strongest and the weakest people in the world. They are naturally endowed with great possibilities, which, when understood and appreciated, take them to supreme heights of strength and usefulness, and when ignored or unrecognized, cause them to be creatures of impulse and fluctuating desire, positively without equilibrium and blown about by every wind of doctrine. In the latter state they are those who constantly seek advice on the simplest subjects, and rarely ever take it; who ask questions with great

THE INFLUENCE OF THE ZODIAC

humility and forget the answers. These persons are aware of possessing unusual power in certain directions, but they are so lazy and so deficient in the ability to concentrate, that these beautiful gifts are scattered and very frequently entirely lost.

Aquarius people are remarkable spiritual healers. Every human being born under this sign possesses this genius, whether he is aware of it or not, and it can be brought into a beautiful and phenomenal use by a respectful and loving recognition. To learn to know opportunity and improve it, is the key to Aquarius' genius.

The Aquarius women are not so timid and apprehensive of danger to those they love as Libra women, or so restless and fidgety as Gemini women, but they usually care more for the acquisition of property than these people, and are apt to be very nervous about their investments, the management of business, and the opinion and speech of people. Those born under this sign are generally very noble, honest, and kind-hearted, and are endowed with considerable natural discrimination. They are fair readers of character, and are not easily deceived by a pitiful tale. This mental and spiritual quickness makes them very apt in any study, any trade, or profession they may take up. It is hardly too much to say that Aquarius men and women who are even partially aware of their power, can succeed in almost any work they may decide to do. They are not rote students, but seem without any particular effort to absorb information from every source. They are always agreeable, and retain their dignity on all occasions. They are rarely passionate or quick tempered, but know how to resent an insult when one is offered.

The Air people are some times unmanageable and not always logical, but they have a comprehension of spiritual cause and effect which is entirely above ordinary material syllogistic reasoning. This power the Aquarius people possess to a remarkable degree, which is the power of inspiration and

THE INFLUENCE OF THE ZODIAC

divination. It is called the Power of the Holy Ghost. When the soul of an Aquarius person is once roused to work for righteousness, improvement is sure to be rapid, and a high spiritual development follows.

All born under this sign have a gift of the spirit which, if they choose to recognize and use, is wonderful indeed. It is the magical ability of controlling insane people. When this fact is generally, as it is privately and scientifically recognized, nurses and guardians of these afflicted people will be chosen from those born under this sign, and they will be carefully trained for the work. The eyes of the silent, quiet, Aquarius person have great hypnotic force, and when the light that shines forth is the light of the Spirit, the ability to heal seems almost superhuman.

PERSONAL APPEARANCE

The general appearance of Aquarius people is that of a tall, fine, dignified, healthy, robust nature, with clear complexion.

COMPANIONS

The truest friends and companions will be found among those born in Aries, Sagittarius, and Aquarius. Aquarius and Libra people sometimes work together most harmoniously.

FAULTS

These people represent the nerves and emotions of the Grand Man, hence are unusually sensitive. As they are the most powerful from a psychological standpoint, they should endeavor fully to comprehend their failings, which are fear, the habit of procrastination, and chronic promise-breaking proclivities. Vacillation and caprice are the despoilers of the genius of this sign.

THE INFLUENCE OF THE ZODIAC

The undeveloped Aquarius individual is sometimes a great braggart and very tiresome in calling attention to aristocracy and pedigree. Their people are the only people on earth, and their friends the ones who are most entitled to attention and deference. They are very fond of titles, and of using in ordinary conversation the prefixes to the names of their intimates. There are some liars found among those born under this sign, but their falsehoods are seldom malicious, as they are born of an overweaning desire to appear to the best advantage, and to raise their friends to a high pinnacle in the estimation of the world. These people usually care too much for personal appearance, and sometimes take great risks to procure for themselves the things they desire. They often bury their higher selves by means of a dogmatic materialism, and a routine of habit which leads to a gloomy and useless life.

DISEASES

The diseases from which these people are most likely to suffer are rheumatism, pains in the head and feet, brain difficulties, low circulation, loss of vital heats, nervous diseases, ending in despondency and gloomy forebodings. All these ailments, and every other known to man, can he entirely dominated, forever cast out, by those who realize that mind is the master, and the body the servant of the mind.

MODE OF GROWTH

The first step of development for those born under this sign is to overcome restlessness and anxiety, to seek only for good in all things, and to be careful not to condemn other people for that which they secretly do themselves. These people should determine to develop their rare gifts, for they are indeed rare and wonderful. They should fight laziness and indifference during every waking hour. They should make no engagements that they do not intend to keep, and they should keep those engagements

THE INFLUENCE OF THE ZODIAC

they do make at the point of the bayonet, if need be. They should work to establish themselves in perfect independence of all outside influences. They should go for advice only to the sanctuary of the Temple of the living God, which is within themselves, where answers are always given to all earnest questions. They should strive with all their might against the power of external things, and never say with their lips the words which the heart contradicts.

Aquarius is the Captain of the Host, who might hold the scepter of the world. Valuable beyond price are hope and trust. Precious beyond words is a life that has no broken promises. To a great soul everything is great. Aquarius, if once you attain the Divine inbreathing with your mighty attuned will, you have only to lift your hands and the world will obey. Your greatest strength lies in triunity. Aquarius people, awake! Be no longer creatures of lost opportunities, of perpetual regrets for what might have been.

MARRIAGE

The children of an Aquarius and Aries marriage are likely to be physically strong and robust, and the domestic relations harmonious, if both husband and wife have learned to overcome their faults. The children of Aquarius and Sagittarius will be high-strung and fine-tempered, but less robust, and the domestic life will be likely to be interesting and full of surprises on account of the quick inspirations of these persons. It can safely be promised that there will be no monotony about it.

These conditions depend muck upon whether the contracting parties are on the same plane of material and social life.

THE INFLUENCE OF THE ZODIAC

GOVERNMENT OF CHILDREN

These children must be taught punctuality and the necessity of keeping promises. They are very easily swayed by those about them. They are finely organized, and possess the faculty of pleasing; when opposed or unkindly treated they become cruel, relentless critics. They will meet honesty and frankness with honesty and frankness, and will prove loyal and faithful to every trust. Doubt them and they will doubt and deceive. They often say harsh things to those they love best, but these things come from the head and not from the heart. They have excellent memories, and by culture can become the most accurate psychometric readers. They should have few companions,and those who are faithful, and patient, and genial. As these children are exceedingly nervous and restless, they should be kept as quiet as possible. Many infants born under this sign have lost their lives by being kept close to a noisy machine-shop or factory.

These little folks should not remain in school against their will, and this is true of all Air and Fire children. When they begin to droop, and dread the atmosphere of the school-room, and lessons become a haunting fear, they should be transferred to the country or allowed to spend most of the waking hours in amusement and outdoor recreation.

The governing planets are Saturn and Uranus; the gems are sapphire, opal, and turquoise; and the astral colors are blue, pink, and Nile green.

THE INFLUENCE OF THE ZODIAC

THE EARTH TRIPLICITY

TAURUS, VIRGO, CAPRICORN

CHAPTER XIV

TAURUS, THE BULL

HEAD SIGN OF THE EARTH TRIPLICITY

April 19 to May 20

This sign governs the neck and throat of the Grand Man, or Macrocosm. It is a fixed, nocturnal, feminine, vernal, earth; sign, and is the positive pole of the Earth Triplicity. The higher attributes are secretion and will. The Sun enters this sign each year on or about April 19. and departs from the sign on or about May 20, The Sun on entering the sign should be gives six days before coming into full touch and action with the influence of the sign. A person born between the dates of the 19th and 25th of April would not receive the full central results of the sign's individuality, as he would he born when the Sun was on the edge of the sign. This is known as the Cusp, and its nature and impulses partake of the sign the Sun has just passed through or out from, and the native will also partake of the attributes of the sign of the Zodiac in which the Moon is located at the time of birth.

This is a very hard sign to overcome. Those born under it are fearless and kind, and very magnanimous when not irritated. They are generous, and apt to load themselves with the burdens and sorrows of others. Money has no special value in their minds except for the good it will do. They have no wish to hoard, and are always ready to divide. They prefer to help with money

THE INFLUENCE OF THE ZODIAC

rather than by the expenditure of time or sympathy. They have great power of concentration, and make the best metaphysical healers. By the power of their will they can project their thought to great distances and hit the mark. They are exceedingly fond of the good things of the earth, and like to spread feasts for their friends. These Taurus individuals are guided far too much by externalities and appearances. The whole physical nature seems to grow out of the five animal senses, but when developed above the sensual appetites they are most powerful mentally and spiritually, making apt writers, and quick, brilliant speakers; in fact, they are very zealous and sanguine in any line of thought they may take up. They often become leaders, and readily adapt themselves to the time and the society which calls them into action. They can memorize with the greatest ease. When friendly, they are very loyal, and remain so as long as they are permitted to rule and have their own way. When they become enemies they are the most hitter and relentless of the whole twelve signs.

Almost all persons horn under Taurus possess some kind of physical mediumship, and are quite apt to be found among Spiritualists who deal in phenomena. Their clairvoyant gifts are usually very marked, and so is the power of independent slate-writing and table-tippings. They feel the minds of other people and know their thoughts.

PERSONAL APPEARANCE

Taurus rules the neck, and that part of the brain that governs the sex principles. Those born under this sign have usually full faces, wide noses and mouths, shining flesh inclined to reddishness, large shoulders, and are generally of powerful build.

COMPANIONS

They will find their best friends and companionships

THE INFLUENCE OF THE ZODIAC

among those born under Capricorn and Libra.

FAULTS

It takes but little to rouse Taurus people to anger, and once excited they are utterly unmanageable. They are not comfortable people to live with when unawakened and undeveloped. They roar and kick under the slightest provocation, and at such times have no regard for feelings or furniture. When so excited they would like to kill. They can never be touched by mental argument or moral suasion when in a passion. Words infuriate them, and the best assistance that can be rendered them is to leave them entirely alone till their wrath has abated, but not in a spirit of resentment. Taurus people are exacting, domineering, and very selfish in their physical demands and expectations. The wives of undeveloped Taurus men are usually very unhappy creatures. These people are sometimes capricious as well as passionate, and the pleasure of today is the bane of tomorrow. Taurus men are hard to cook for, and Taurus women are hypercritical in all domestic matters, as they consider that their way is the best way and the only way. Those born under this sign would like to dominate the world, but their interference in other people's affairs often causes them to be much disliked.

DISEASES

The diseases to which these people are subject are morbid mental conditions, heart troubles, dropsy, and tumors; when sensuality rules, apoplexy and brain disorders result. All these ailments and every other known to man can be entirely dominated, forever cast out, by those who realize that mind is the master and the body the servant of mind.

MODE OF GROWTH

Those born under this sign should learn silence and

THE INFLUENCE OF THE ZODIAC

patience as a daily exercise. They should never talk of self, and should school the mind to look upon the opposite sex so as never to be lost in sex passions. Without this training, a diseased imagination is sure to grow, which will overwhelm the male, and bring disaster and ruin to the female. If Taurus individuals will overcome their passions and be honest and truthful to their better natures, they can perform a mighty work. To know the right, yet to dally with the wrong, is the philosophy of death. They should remember that the "greatest of all conquests is the conquest of self." They are open to all the new discoveries of human progress and hope, and can have at command vast intellectual power. They should be alone as much as possible, for they are natural psychic collectors of thought adapted for present material use. They also must learn to make all important decisions when entirely alone, because they are influenced by those around them. They must keep free from anger and jealousy. The female should use the utmost care to guard against being led away, or misled through sympathetic feeling or flattery.

The most dangerous and violent types of the animal Taurus and the animal man Taurus have been subjugated by the spirit of love. Valuable bulls, which nothing could subdue, have been instantly soothed and led captive by children who love them, and in whom they have confidence. And so with the animal man. Taurus people should avoid all stimulating food and drink. Many murderers are found among the men who inflame their native passions by the use of alcoholic stimulants. All born under this sign should strive to possess their own souls and find the path of silence which leads to the Temple of Peace. They should remember that "he that ruleth his spirit is greater than he who taketh a city."

MARRIAGES

The union of those born under Taurus and Capricorn is apt to be harmonious, and the children of these signs physically

THE INFLUENCE OF THE ZODIAC

strong and robust. Next come Taurus and Libra, and the children of such union will be very bright intellectually, with very few exceptions. Where Taurus is united with those born under other signs, the children are not likely to live; find happiness in seldom realized. These conditions depend much upon whether the contracting parties are on the same plane of material and social life.

GOVERNMENT OF CHILDREN

As a rule, most children born under this sign are willful and determined to have their own way at all hazards. They have great power of endurance, and are natural conquerors. They are very quick to follow the example of older associates, and should be carefully guarded in such respects. Although these little folks are stubborn, they are easily turned aside when governed by a strong, loving hand. They must be taught truthfulness and allegiance to law above all things. They are selfish, and when permitted to have their own way, become very unyielding and indifferent to the trouble and suffering they inflict upon others. A tremendous amount of vitality pertains to this sign, and much trouble is often caused by overeating. Such indulgence has a pernicious effect upon the sex appetites, which are apt to show themselves early in Taurus children, ending in disaster and ruin. They must be taught kindness and sympathy for all domestic animals; cruelty to household pets may end in a wicked desire to destroy human life. There is a constant menace to all Taurus children who are permitted to grow into a life of self-gratification. These little ones are often maliciously untruthful. Falsehood is a constant weapon for the accomplishment of their desires. They will also appropriate the property of others, and must constantly watched and checked they become very bold and exceedingly destructive.

The governing planet is Venus, and the gems are moss-agate and emerald. The astral colors are red and lemon-yellow.

THE INFLUENCE OF THE ZODIAC

CHAPTER XV

VIRGO, THE VIRGIN

MIDDLE SIGN OF THE EARTH TRIPLICITY

August 22 to September 23

This sign governs the bowels, the solar-plexus, and the spleen of the Grand Man, or Macrocosm. It is an earthy, feminine, nocturnal, human, speaking, dry, common sign of the Zodiac. The higher attributes are circulation and vibration. The Sun enters the sign each year on or about the 22nd of August and departs from the sign on or about September 23rd The Sun on entering the sign should be given six days before coming into full touch and action with the influence of the sign. A person born between the dates of the 22nd and the 28th of September would not receive the full central results of the sign's individuality, as be would be born when the Sun was on the edge of the sign. This is known as the Cusp, and its nature and impulses partake of the sign the Sun has just passed through and out from, and the native will also partake of the attributes of the sign of the Zodiac in which the Moon is located at the time of birth.

This sign represents the bidden fire of the earth. People born under it are very orderly and methodical, and are good magnetic healers. Their hands seem charged with curative power. They are generous, and very solicitous about other people's affairs. They are usually much interested in the love matters of their friends, and have little hesitation in making or breaking matches. They are fine scholars, and make inspirational musicians. They keep their own secrets, and guard the secrets of their friends with equal fidelity. They are capable and efficient in all they undertake, being excellent planners and designers. The

THE INFLUENCE OF THE ZODIAC

women are particularly fastidious about their dress, and like to lead the fashion. They are affectionate and devoted in the family, and are strong believers in blue blood. They aspire to the best things, but are easily discouraged in their climbing. These people are natural philosophers, and possess the most accurate intellectual discrimination of the whole twelve signs of the Zodiac. They are capable of reaching great heights as writers, public speakers, and musicians; they are natural chemists, and often excel as newspaper editors, from their knowledge of the reading public. They rebound quickly from defeat or disaster, because having great endurance and aptitude they can surmount almost every difficulty. As proof-readers they are exceedingly accurate. Their natural impulses are materialistic, and their deductions are usually drawn from the external, material side of things. Once they cross the threshold of the spiritual domain, they make rapid headway, and soon comprehend the principles of soul and spirit, becoming true teachers of the philosophy of human life and the immortality of the soul. The sense of feeling and touch is very accurate in these people, and by practice and drilling they quickly develop rare psychometric gifts. With proper training, these Virgo people may grow into the most powerful spiritual physicians. When entirely on the intellectual plane, they are crucial in their criticisms, and often become arbitrary and selfish, expecting perfection. Order and harmony are very necessary to their health. Food will not do them much good if anger and strife abound.

PERSONAL APPEARANCE

Virgo people are usually of middle or tallish stature, well formed, with oval face, a musical voice, and elegant manner.

COMPANIONS

True companionship will be found among those born under Libra or Sagittarius, and those who come under their own

THE INFLUENCE OF THE ZODIAC

sign, Virgo.

FAULTS

The faults of Virgo people consist in their domineering tendencies, interference with other people's affairs, and the freedom with which they criticize the faults and shortcomings of others. They have generally an overweaning respect for money and position, and many imitators and toadies are to be found among those who have not learned to overcome this false pride and ambition. Dollars and cents have a value quite apart from the comforts and pleasures they provide. These are distinguishing marks which elevate their possessors to the most enviable attitudes.

Virgo people are usually firm believers in the necessity of medicine, and seem to be the victims of all sorts of maladies, if they are judged by their own accounts of their symptoms. They are usually very constant to physicians, often changing their aches, but not their doctors. Those born under this sign should not take drugs, for they never need them. In fact, they should keep clear of strong medicine and physicians. Nature is their unfailing remedy. They are apt to pick everything and everybody to pieces, and because of this analytical tendency are a great discouragement to others, especially those who are not talented in giving the reason for the faith that is in them. Air and Fire people are often every much irritated by those born under Virgo, and sometimes Virgo people do not get along well together for the same reason. Virgo people will confess to almost every fault except the ones they possess. These they do not seem to be aware of, and generally repudiate every intention to wound or hurt by their merciless criticisms. They are the individuals who feel called upon to tell disagreeable truths to people "for their good."

They are prone to prophesy, but as they reason from the objective and external, their prophecies often fail. This

THE INFLUENCE OF THE ZODIAC

admiration of Virgo people for externals, and the desire to make a good appearance, lead some of them into habits of exaggeration and falsehood, and frequently into debt, from which extrication seems almost impossible. Virgo is the one sign of the Zodiac which is credited with an almost total immunity from disease, and yet Virgo people are those who are apt to be experimenting with drugs and physicians, and they seldom need either, even when living on what may be termed a purely animal plane. They are usually restored from fatigue or the appearance of illness by a few hours with nature. Green grass and swaying trees, and the beauty, harmony, and utility of vegetable and animal life are their infallible remedies. Both the men and women born under this sign retain their freshness and youth to a remarkable degree. There is very little change in the appearance of a Virgo person endowed with ordinary common sense from thirty to sixty years. Those who are so ignorant as to dose themselves perpetually, and who are intemperate in eating and drinking, do not of course come under this head. But to Virgo seems to have been given eternal youth.

DISEASES

There are certain stomach troubles and nervous conditions assigned those born under Virgo who are careless and neglectful of themselves. They can have them or not as they choose.

The author is of the firm opinion that the last statement is true of every person born into the world who has intelligence enough to realize that spirit is master and matter the servant. Intelligence is the infallible cure for sin, suffering, disease, and death.

THE INFLUENCE OF THE ZODIAC

MODE OF GROWTH

Their mode of growth is by the endeavor to realize that there is nothing perfect in nature, and to become alive to their own failings- their real faults and not their alleged ones. They should lay bare their inmost selves to the magnifying glass which they are so fond of using with others. They should endeavor to realize that an unkind comment or a hasty, cruel criticism is harder to bear and more lasting in its effects than a physical hurt or blow. They should learn to judge others by themselves in such matters. They should try to give credit and praise to truth, virtue, and real merit, instead of rendering homage to money, aristocratic appearances, and the superficialities of life. They should not he ashamed of honest work. There are women born under this sign who would feel permanently disgraced by being caught in the act of washing dishes or sweeping a room. These are the people who whisper and strive to hide their economies and financial inabilities. They should struggle to be frank, and to be less sensitive to public opinion.

When once those born under this sign become aware that there is something besides the pleasures that arise from money and intellectual pursuits, they grow spiritually very fast, and the natural analytical tendency which made them so disagreeable, so hard to get along with, becomes a great power for good. When this keen intellectual discrimination is |vitalized by spiritual love and the desire to help, which is love's distinguishing characteristic, these Virgo people are very reliable and inspiring. They can attain to great heights and draw many to them because of a naturally strong magnetic influence, which increases as the impulse to rise develops.

MARRIAGES

Harmony will be likely to prevail when Virgo people

THE INFLUENCE OF THE ZODIAC

unite with those in their own sign. Brilliant children, but not over strong, will be the result when united in marriage with persons in Libra. Marked genius and originality result when united with Sagittarius people. It must be remembered that harmony will be more apt to exist where the marital union is with those who are on or about on the same social or intellectual plane.

GOVERNMENT OF CHILDREN

The children born under this sign are the true children of Nature. They have strong likes and dislikes, with a dominant will power, quick discrimination and understanding, and very early in life show a talent for a business career. Their attention should never be called to the evil in the world, or to the faults of their companions, as this is very apt to prove a contamination which will embitter the whole life. They should be continually instructed to look for the good in other people, and for the pure and beautiful in every thing. The tendency to critical analysis is the distinguishing trait of this sign, and the children are quick to form the habit of unkind judgment. They are natural students. Give them a small garden to plant, to watch, and to attend to the seedlings. Give them music as a recreation and a presence of harmony. This will be a kindly force and elegance of taste which bring hope and joy to the household. They have a very sensitive skin, and must be filly trained as to bathing. These children should never be given drugs of any kind. Good pure air, with full breath exercises and harmonious metaphysical treatments are the true natural medicines for Virgo people.

The governing planet is Mercury, and the gems are pink jasper and hyacinth. Astral colors are gold and black, with speckled blue dots.

THE INFLUENCE OF THE ZODIAC

CHAPTER XVI

CAPRICORN, THE GOAT

THE LAST SIGN OF THE EARTH TRIPLICITY

December 21 to January 20

This sign governs the knees and the hams of the Grand Man, or Macrocosm, and is a dry, earthy, feminine, nocturnal, southern, changeable, domestic sign of the Zodiac, the negative pole of the Earth Triplicity. The higher attributes are absorption and inspiration. The Sim enters the sign Capricorn on or about the 21st of December of each year, and departs from the sign on or about the 20th of January. The Sun on entering the sign should be given six days before coming into full touch and action with the influence of the sign. A person born between the dates of the 21st and the 27th of December would not receive the full central results of the sign's individuality, as he would be born when the Sun was on the edge of the sign. This is known as the Cusp, and its nature and impulses partake of the sign the Sun has just passed through and out from, and the native will also partake of the attributes of the sign of the Zodiac in which the Moon is located at the date of birth.

This sign represents the dark side of the earth, the occult side of history, solitude, and meditation. People born under it are deep thinkers, natural orators, and teachers. They are worshipers of intellect, and devotees to book knowledge. They are insatiable in their desire for intellectual growth. They are indefatigable workers, and apt to tire quickly because they usually do several things at a time. Like the goat, they will work for themselves without stop or stint, but are very restless when harnessed to work for others. They are not overstocked with self-esteem, and are apt to be self-conscious. Capricorn people resent all

THE INFLUENCE OF THE ZODIAC

interference, and never meddle with the affairs of others. They are fine entertainers, have excellent memories, and excel in story telling. This is the most brilliant and the most depressed sign in the Zodiac. When jolly, these Capricorners are very jolly; when miserable, they are more miserable than all the others put together, and can usually give no adequate reason for their wretchedness. They are kind-hearted, loyal, secretive. A friend once is a friend always. They are usually careful in all money and business affairs, and a promise is sacredly regarded. They are natural planners, and know bow to make both ends meet.

The majority of the people born under this sign are natural absorbents of natural laws, and are efficient servers to the vast body of humanity in a material way. They are adapted to the carrying out of large projects, and have wonderful continuity in attending to any enterprise which promises handsome material benefits; but they are apt to lose heart when the outlook seems small. Every Capricorn person should have a good business education and a practical experience in self-maintenance, even if they are prospective heirs or heiresses. These people are very particular about appearances, and set a great value upon the opinion of the world. The desire to keep pace with the aristocracy has ruined many a Capricorn individual. The women are usually far more discreet financial managers than the men, and are very careful housekeepers, possessing much taste in the arrangement as well as the management of the home. They are often able to take charge of hotels and institutions where many servants are employed. Some excellent musicians come from this sign. When the individual is born so as to be marked by the sign before Capricorn (Sagittarius), on the Cusp, as it is called, the gift of prophecy is likely to be most marked. Some of the most successful actors and actresses are the result of this combination of signs. Capricorn people are proud, high-minded, determined, independent, lovers of harmony and beauty, but apt to live too much in externals. They are the people of great material aspirations.

THE INFLUENCE OF THE ZODIAC

Capricorn people are sometimes very indiscreet and very eccentric in their charities and investments. They are apt to be prodigal in giving and buying, and they are also very close in these matters. This seems to depend upon the mood. When the spirits are high and the world looks green, there seems no end to material resources; but when the darkness descends, and this is likely to be a frequent occurrence, "the rainy day" turns up and there is no pleasure in purchasing or giving. Occasionally a Capricorn individual will be found who is not subject to fits of depression. When this is the case, the sanguine temperament predominates so thoroughly that the "rainy day" is seldom anticipated. Indeed these exceptions are generally reckless in money matters.

These people are the most natural teachers to be found in any sign, and this is because they are patient with details. They do not expect the child of seven to know as much as the child of double that age. Then they are very practical in this work, and generally very kind. The pupils of these Capricorn individuals are always devoted to them, and have a great desire to progress, if for no other reason than to please the instructor. These people abhor flattery, but are exceedingly appreciative of the commendation which they feel they have righteously earned. They are magnetic, and draw people to them by the working of a natural law, but they dislike any especial demonstration of affection. They know when they are really liked, and this knowledge is quite sufficient. Indeed, there is no worse torture for these persons than to be compelled by courtesy to submit to kisses and caresses. Only to those they really love are they in the least demonstrative. When awakened and developed, they become the most zealous and unwearied workers in spiritual things. To raise them from the apathy which a long experience in external life has fostered is a difficult matter, but when roused they seem to be wider awake than the people of almost any other domain.

THE INFLUENCE OF THE ZODIAC

PERSONAL APPEARANCE

They are generally short of stature, and sometimes have very dark complexions and dark hair, with exceedingly expressive eyes.

COMPANIONS

The most congenial friends and companions will be found with those born in Taurus, Virgo, and Libra, or those born about the same time of year as themselves.

FAULTS

The faults of these people are selfishness and self-distrust. They talk too much, and magnify their troubles and perplexities. The spiritual nature is hard to reach, but once aroused is capable of the highest development. They are not quick to anger, but when their rights are meddled with they can be passionate and cruel in their denunciations.

DISEASES

The disease most likely to attack those born under this sign are indigestion and melancholia. They are often the victims of overwork because of their determination to achieve brilliantly whatever they undertake, and because of their lack of judgment in reference to their powers of endurance.

These ailments and all others known to man, can he entirely dominated, forever cast out, by those who realize that mind is the master and the body the servant of the mind.

THE INFLUENCE OF THE ZODIAC

MODE OF GROWTH

As these people talk too much, they should first learn silence and deep meditation, and search for the best methods of overcoming the habit of unkind judgment. They should learn discrimination about methods of work, and not ruin their fine powers by a too strict adherence to precedent and public opinion. They should make a careful study of themselves, find their weakest points, and then set diligently to work to strengthen them. The chief lesson for an intelligent Capricorn person to learn is that there is something higher than the intellect, and that there are things which cannot be proved by mathematics or worked out by a syllogism. When the teachers in this sign are illuminated by spiritual light their power for good is unlimited, and they seem to possess every gift worth having. This light can be obtained only by looking up and away from self. The tendency to morbid introspection and the habit of dwelling upon the ills of life make this a difficult matter. The earth's attraction for these people is very strong, but it is often beautifully overcome. There is great credit in such conquest, for this sign represents the dark side of the earth, called by some Hades.

MARRIAGES

The happiest unions will be found between Capricorn and Taurus persons, and the off-spring will be strong physically. More intellectual children will result when Capricorn is united with Libra, and a greater endowment of power and genius will accrue to the off- spring of Capricorn and Virgo.

GOVERNMENT OF CHILDREN

Children born under this sign should not be associated with cross or coarse people, as they readily take on the conditions of those about them. Great care should he taken to

THE INFLUENCE OF THE ZODIAC

instruct them in a plain matter-of-fact understanding of the uses and the abuses of the sex nature.

It is impossible to be too earnest in this education, nor can they be too early impressed with the realities of human life, and the necessity of self-government, especially in the matter of pride. These Capricorn children are inclined to he haughty and arrogant if not controlled. Like their elders who have not been brought into harmony with spiritual truth, they reason from external, material standpoints, and are apt to feel that they know it all. To make these children willing servers, unwearied pains should be taken to cultivate in them a desire to serve others rather than themselves. It is also vitally necessary that they be taught discretion in eating. Unwearied pains should be taken to keep these children simple in their desires and natural in behavior, as the tendency of this sign is toward outward display, which very soon degenerates into vulgar and shoddy tastes.

This sign is governed by Saturn, and the gems are white onyx, and moonstone. The astral colors are garnet, brown, silver-gray, and black.

THE INFLUENCE OF THE ZODIAC

THE WATER TRIPLICITY

CANCER, SCORPIO, PISCES

CHAPTER XVII

CANCER, THE CRAB

HEAD SIGN OF THE WATER TRIPLICITY

June 21 to July 22

This sign governs the breast and maternal functions of the Grand Man or Macrocosm. It is a cardinal, feminine, movable, watery, phlegmatic, nocturnal sign, the positive Pole of the Water Triplicity, The higher attributes are feeling and sympathy. The Sun enters the sign each year or on about the 21st of June, and departs from it on or about the 22nd of July. The Sun on entering the sign should be given six days before coming into full touch and action with the influence of the sign. A person born between the dates of the 21st and the 27th of June would not receive the full central results of the sign's individuality, as he would be born when the Sun was on the edge of the sign. This is known as the Cusp, and its nature and impulses partake of the sign the Sun has just passed through or out from, and the native will also partake of the attributes of the sign of the Zodiac the Moon is located in at the time of birth.

This sign is called the paradox of the twelve. A few harmonious people are to be found in it, who as far as known have not given any especial attention to mental or spiritual development; but, generally speaking, the genius of the Cancer sign is exceedingly difficult to explain. Those born under it have a persistent will, a dutch of determination, intuition, and purpose.

THE INFLUENCE OF THE ZODIAC

Yet they often let go for a slight reason, or for no apparent reason. They are invincible to argument, and cannot be talked out of a thing; but if their feelings are hurt, they are apt to lose heart, and abandon whatever they have undertaken. Their great sensitiveness leads them into the most absurd extremes. They are as strong as giants and as weak as infants. These people are fond of travel, often taking long voyages, which are not always successful.

Those born under Cancer will be gifted in many directions far above the average, if educated thoroughly. They have a very superior intelligence, and an aptitude for learning new things and working out new principles. They are generous and full of sympathy for the public good, but they demand a full independence to develop the same. They are often capricious, and frequently change their occupation. Cancer people who have not given themselves to the work of development are apt to talk of the personal self, and this tendency becomes a habit which grows into disease in mature life. It is very hard for them to work under the direction of others, and correspondingly difficult for them to live harmoniously in a house that they are not at the head of. They are ardent lovers of home, and have fine executive ability in its management, and are devoted to their children. Notwithstanding their love and loyalty, those born under this sign are apt to change companions and friends very frequently, often becoming bitter enemies of those to whom they were previously attached. They are tactful to diplomacy in some matters, and show their hands with painful clearness in others. Their powers of understanding are very quick and keen; and they have excellent memories. Among them are indefatigable scholars and some of our finest public speakers. Both the men and women are very fond of money; the male is apt to become miserly, the female covetous and ambitious to get and board. These are the people who are afraid and ashamed of poverty, who count their silver, and hide their gems in stockings, and who are in constant expectation of burglars.

THE INFLUENCE OF THE ZODIAC

The mind of the Cancer person is mechanical. The men usually succeed well in manufacturing business and active trade of all kinds. The women are intellectual, are often very logical writers and speakers, remarkably progressive in their ideas, and frequently found among the prime movers in great humane enterprises.

The Cancer people are very apt to be comfortable, happy, and unassailable during the day, but very unhappy and depressed at night. They are conscientious about giving advice, and like to be consulted in important matters. They are kind in illness and trouble, and devoted and efficient when the responsibility rests upon them. They are very tenacious of their own and their children's rights, and very courageous in defending them. They are fond of the beautiful and artistic, and like to be handsomely attired. They are neat and orderly and expect everybody else to be. The Cancer men are far more constant than the Cancer women.

PERSONAL APPEARANCE

These people are usually of medium stature, rather large in the upper portion of the body, with round face, soft skin, tawny or very pale complexion, small features, and light or grayish eyes. They are apt to be weak in constitution.

COMPANIONS

Their congenial companionship will be found with those born in Pisces and Scorpio. The offspring will be the strongest when a Cancer and a Pisces person are united.

FAULTS

Their faults are laziness, selfishness, jealousy, vanity, and love of money for money's sake and for purposes of display.

THE INFLUENCE OF THE ZODIAC

The undeveloped Cancer woman will go to great lengths to obtain the garments and jewels which her really fine taste covets beyond anything else in the world. These women like to wear sparkling gems, and are always striving to show them to the best advantage. The men, as well as the women, are inordinately fond of seeing their names in print, and are always seeking the plaudits of the mob. They can be very cruel and vindictive, and are quick to resent a personal criticism. The women are exceedingly fickle and inconstant, and on this account are seldom happily married. They exact constancy in others, and appear to he quite unaware of their own dereliction in this respect. They claim to be the paragons of truth, but are inclined to much fabrication. Cancer is the only sign of the Zodiac governed the Moon, and the changeable qualities of the people are attributed to its influence.

DISEASES

The diseases likely to attack these people are weak digestion and gastric troubles. These ailments and every other known to man can he entirely dominated, forever cast out, by those who realize that mind is the master and the body the servant of mind.

MODE OF GROWTH

As these people have great aptitude in learning new things, they should give themselves to such study as will strengthen the will and enlighten the conscience. Spiritual and metaphysical subjects should he taken up, and the substitution of the true for the false, the reality for the sham, should be religiously attempted. Women who are fond of their diamonds should wear no diamonds; they should set themselves to the work of cultivating the inner life by turning their backs upon externalities and personalities, especially masculine personalities. They should strive for loyalty, constancy, nobility

THE INFLUENCE OF THE ZODIAC

in all matters. They should put a bridle on their tongues, and cultivate respect as well as toleration for other people's opinions.

MARRIAGE

Those born under this sign should never marry early in life; in fact, a single life is generally to be preferred for the Cancer women. They should study themselves most conscientiously in this vital matter. When these people are unhappy in the marital relation, they are not only the most wretched people in the world, but they are the most dangerous, as their caprice will lead them to an utter disregard of all advice and the feelings of the nearest and dearest. They see no reason for being bound in an uncongenial relation, and if they cannot break it in one way they will in another.

Domestic happiness is possible to those born under this sign who have made a study of self and learned to govern self. But the true talent of these people will usually be best understood and subserved by a single life.

GOVERNMENT OF CHILDREN

The greatest care should be taken with Cancer children, and their training and development should commence very early. Their exceeding sensitiveness makes them hard to manage, although these little ones are very obliging and gentle if properly treated. They are sympathetic with sorrow and suffering, but inclined to dwell upon the abnormal aspects of these conditions, and to grow very nervous and excited when describing them.

The attention of these children should be turned in babyhood to the contemplation of the true, the sweet, the tender, the harmonious. They should not be taken to funerals, nor made to spend much time with people who are very ill. They should always be dressed simply, no matter what the social position or condition of the parents. To overdress a Cancer girl is sometimes to ruin her for life. In every possible way the attention of the young should be turned to the attainment of "a meek and quiet spirit." It is an especially good plan to have regular times for these little ones to sit perfectly still and perfectly silent. Five minutes three or four times a day will be of the greatest assistance in their development. Such periods of forced rest from all activity of tongue and limb are very helpful for the restless, nervous, and talkative children of every sign.

The proper development of Cancer children is often seriously retarded by over-fond parents, nurses, and guardians, who insist upon clasping them close to themselves. These electromagnetic conditions are annoying, exciting, and very debilitating to the nervous system, No child should sleep with old people, but this is particularly true of Cancer children, who very easily depleted and made ill. No pains should be spared to familiarize these children with the laws of life, and especially with those governing the sex functions, special care should be given to their diet their hours of rest and sleep.

With care and consideration, these children can be brought to a spiritually harmonious manhood and womanhood, and, when this is accomplished, there are no stronger, more brilliant, or more useful people than those who stand at the head of the Water Triplicity.

The governing planet is the Moon, and the gems are emerald and black onyx. The astral colors ore green and russet brown.

THE INFLUENCE OF THE ZODIAC

CHAPTER XVIII

SCORPIO, THE SCORPION

MIDDLE SIGN OF THE WATER TRIPLICITY

October 23 to November 22

This sign governs the genital organs, the groins, bladder, and sex functions of the Grand Man, or Macrocosm, It is a fixed, nocturnal, southern, mute sign of the Zodiac. The higher attributes are attachment, tenacity, and silence. The Sun enters the sign on or about the 23rd of October, and departs from the sign on or about the 22nd of November. The Sun on entering the sign should be given six days before coming into full touch and action with the influence of the sign. A person born between the dates of the 23rd and the 29th of October would not receive the full central results of the sign's individuality, as he would be born when the Sun was on the edge of the sign. This is known as the Cusp, and its nature and impulses partake of the sign the Sun has just passed through and out from, and the native will also partake of the attributes of the sign of the Zodiac the Moon is located in at the time of birth.

These people are allied to the great powers of the ocean of this planet, and are possessed of a wonderful vibratory force, which gives them a great vitality through electro-magnetic influences. So marked is this power that they are able to benefit all who are closely connected with them. Their personal presence is a healing. They possess indomitable will and self control, and remarkable skill in the use of their hands. Their touch is so firm and delicate, their observation so keen, their poise so perfect, that they make the best surgeons in the world. They are not moved by the complaints or fears of their patients, and preserve the coolness of their native element under all circumstances,

THE INFLUENCE OF THE ZODIAC

however trying. Such persons are often considered unfeeling and unsympathetic, and this is sometimes true, though more frequently is an appearance caused by a resolute and unflinching determination to succeed. Before an operation some of these surgeons are regarded by their patients as demons. Afterwards they are always gods. The genius of eloquence is sometimes a direct inheritance of those born under this sign. They are powerful and magnetic public speakers, and when the spiritual nature is aroused they make the most popular and convincing clergymen. They have great tact and taste in the choice of language, and are usually very well aware of their influence over those with whom they come in contact, Those who write excel in the construction of short stories. One strong characteristic of these people is a silent, dignified superiority of appearance. This is a very important factor in their success. They are usually courteous and affable when not engaged in serious business; then they can be blunt to cruelty. They are fond of the good things of the earth, and have a fine taste in dress, but are not so devoted to style and show as their Cancer neighbors. They are especially fond of outdoor sports, and are natural lovers of ocean travel and ocean views. When these people are awakened and spiritualized, they are the salt of the earth, helpful, powerful, tender, and devoted to humanity. The reverse of this is also true. They usually have so much business of their own to carry to success that they are not curious concerning the affairs of their neighbors. They have large self-esteem and approbativeness to match. Flattery is the most powerful weapon that can be used with the average Scorpio person.

PERSONAL APPEARANCE

Those born under this sign are usually robust, and inclined to corpulence in middle life. They have dusky complexions, broad, square faces, and dark hair.

THE INFLUENCE OF THE ZODIAC

COMPANIONS

The best companionships exist with those born under Pisces, the negative pole of the Water Triplicity. Stanch friends are to be found in Libra and in Virgo.

FAULTS

Three great evils are apt to dominate Scorpio people when on the animal plane. These are anger, jealousy, and passion, and if permitted to hold sway will destroy their integrity and ruin their lives. This sign is the natural propagative center, and the unawakened Scorpio person is sometimes a monster of lust. The intense love of praise and flattery is another great weakness. The husband who does not coax and praise his Scorpio wife has not infrequently a very hard time of it. The education of the male has been different, therefore they are not always so exacting in small things, but when their suspicion and jealousy are fully aroused they want to kill, and sometimes do. The habit of procrastination and indolence are very marked, and if not broken become veritable diseases. Those who have not learned the higher law of love are often very unsatisfactory and eccentric in their dealings with their friends, A friend is a splendid fellow as long as he can be used, but when he no longer contributes to their happiness and well-being, he will be tossed aside with no more compunction than one would throw away a squeezed lemon. Later, if they feel that the assistance of the enemy is necessary, the bridge will be rebuilt and used to the utmost. Scorpio people have infinite tact in such matters, and their wonderful magnetic power enables them to destroy and restore these friendships with, ease and grace.

When Scorpio people live on the higher plane, they are very superior individuals; when they do not, they are apt to be tricky, subtle, and very cunning. They have a way of finding out

THE INFLUENCE OF THE ZODIAC

secrets, and especially those which pertain to business and social successes. Information thus gained is always utilized to the beat advantage, and if it decreases the income or the power of the friend, it is regarded as a good joke by the one who has used the information thus fraudulently obtained. These unawakened Scorpio people will atop at nothing to attain their ends on account of their determination and persistence. Whether working for good or evil results, they are indefatigable in their efforts to accomplish their purposes.

The women in this sign who have not learned to control themselves are apt to be great scolds and the worst naggers in the world. Their children are usually the especial victims. Such women are so jealous and auspicious of their husbands, and so fearful that other women will have some power over them, that they are constantly on the watch for an appearance of infidelity. A smile or a look is sometimes sufficient to cause a serious domestic storm. When this suspicion keeps up, separations and divorces are sure to follow. These people will lie just to make mischief. The undeveloped Scorpio man is very hard to live with peaceably. He will also nag, and pick things and motives to pieces, and throw the whole family into a state of nervousness and fear.

DISEASES

The diseases which are apt to attack these people are those of the heart, weakness of the back, lumbago, and gout. All these ailments and every other known man can be entirely dominated, forever cast out, by those who realize that mind is master and the body is the servant of the mind.

MODE OF GROWTH

Scorpio people should remember that one true friend is preferable to a hundred flatterers, and that true friends are very

THE INFLUENCE OF THE ZODIAC

rare, for the reason that true men and women are not common. They should begin at once to take account of their tendencies and their weaknesses. They should set apart a few moments each day for searching, analytical mental contemplation, and not spare themselves. They should resolve with all the splendid will-power and determination which belongs to this sign to overcome every obstacle to true spiritual progress. These people can be anything they choose to be, and while their faults are difficult to overcome, they are so superiorly endowed with resolution that they can succeed if they will. If they could but catch a glimpse of their possibilities of the work they could do in the world, of their magnetic, curative, and inspirational powers they possess, they would never lag in the work of redemption. They must overcome suspicion and jealousy, and this can be only accomplished by the realization of the existence of these damaging and despoiling qualities. They must acknowledge that they are prone to excuse themselves, and, worse than this, to flatten themselves. Some of the Scorpio people who read this will immediately protest. "No such faults are mine," they will say, and perhaps in their indignation will close the book and vow never to have anything more to do with it. Such an exhibition of temper will prove that they are well hit, because those born under this sign who have given no attention to spiritual development are always very tender of their own feelings and equally careless of the suffering of others.

This may be true of other signs, for Scorpio people are not the only ones who wish to deceive themselves.

The women who indulge in scolding and nagging will do well to notice the effect of such conduct upon those about them. They will see that it drives away from them those they love the most and for whose real good they are most anxious. It will not take long for them to discover that their children and all under their authority are deceiving and evading their commands. Servants to such mistresses, unless very conscientious,

THE INFLUENCE OF THE ZODIAC

invariably do things their own way, and become very tactful and cunning. When Scorpio people step to the moral plane where they will acknowledge their faults, the battle is half won, but as long as they determine to deceive themselves they are in utter darkness.

MARRIAGE

When Scorpio and Virgo people are united, the children will be physically strong and brilliant, and when the contracting parties have learned the happiness and power obtained from overcoming, a wonderful harmony will result. The children of Libra and Scorpio, or Scorpio and Pisces, are not apt to be robust, and the marriage relation is usually a marriage in name only.

The reader must remember that usually the happiest results arise in marriage where social and intellectual equality exist.

GOVERNMENT OF CHILDREN

The little folks born under Scorpio are usually very domineering, and evince this tendency even in babyhood. They are the fretting those who demand instant attention, and who expect to be constantly amused. The Scorpio child who has not learned something of self-control, and who has not been instructed concerning the danger of giving way to jealousy and suspicion before he or she has come to the age of ten years, will not be easily reached during the next ten. Moral and spiritual development will then be an individual matter entirely, and it will come from the working out of a natural law- the hardest and the only one- "As a man soweth that shall he also reap."

These children are generally so bright, so apt, so quick to separate the good from the bad, the true from the false, when

THE INFLUENCE OF THE ZODIAC

properly trained and directed, that they can be saved a great deal of after misery and shame by wise instruction in the very early years. This is of course true in the largest sense of all children, but these Scorpio little folks will by their natural tendency to dominate every thing and everybody about them unless this characteristic is corrected as soon as the trait manifests itself. Scorpio babies should be taught to entertain themselves, and should be kept very quiet.

The largest and highest possible range of education should be given those born under this sign. These children are usually very fond of animals, but sometimes become extremely cruel when their commands are not obeyed. They should be led into a close intimacy with these dumb creatures as soon as they are old enough to notice, by means of pictures and a personal acquaintance. Scorpio children are very fond of luxurious surroundings. They should be taught simplicity in all things, and carefully watched as to emotion and passionate habits. This field is worthy most patient and persistent working.

The governing planet is Mars, and the gems are topaz and malachite. The astral colors are golden brown, and black.

THE INFLUENCE OF THE ZODIAC

CHAPTER XIX

PISCES, THE FISHES

LAST SIGN OF THE WATER TRIPLICITY

February 19 to March 21

This sign governs the feet of the Grand Man, or Macrocosm. It is a phlegmatic, nocturnal, common, effeminate, watery sign, the negative pole of the Water Triplicity. The higher attributes are emotion and silence. The Sun enters the sign on or about the 19th of February, and departs from it on or about the 21st of March. The Sim on entering the sign should be given six days before coming into full touch and action with the influence of the sign. A person born between the dates of the 19th and the 25th of February would not receive the full central results of the sign's individuality, as he would be born when the Sun was on the edge of the sign. This is known as the Cusp, and its nature and impulses partake of the sign the Sun has just passed through and out from, and the native will also partake of the attributes of the sign of the Zodiac the Moon is located in at the time of birth. This is called the Metaphysical Sign of Understanding.

These people have a deep, hidden love-nature, and are always anxious to give of their abundance to all who need. They are natural lovers, and their realm is the kingdom of the soul. They rarely look for dishonesty; on the contrary, are prone to have too much confidence in the words and praises of those they love. They are very loyal to their friends, and will defend them whether right or wrong, It is almost impossible for the average Pisces person to acknowledge a flaw in the person cared for. These are the people who will deny themselves the absolute comforts of life to further the interests of relative or friend. These are also the people of quick attractions and equally quick

THE INFLUENCE OF THE ZODIAC

repulsions, though they are generally too kind to let their aversions be seen. They are very fond of beautiful things in nature and art, and among them are to be found excellent art critics, artists, and writers. They have a limpid purity of style when properly educated, that resembles the clear, blue, shimmering water which is their native element. When writing, they have always an eye to the placidly picturesque. These Pisces people are also very magnetic, and some splendid healers are to be found among them. Their gift seems to be the peculiar and sacred one of laying on of hands. In this beautiful work their great desire to help often causes them to give too much, and consequently to deplete and injure themselves.

These people are rarely satisfied with giving. They will empty their pockets and spend all the vital force they have on hand, and then fret because they have not done more. Those born under this sign do not demand quite so much as they give; if they did they would be the most difficult people on earth to live with. They are naturally very honest and clean-minded, and the women are easily disgusted with anything coarse or common. In marriage they become very unhappy if the relation is degraded into a merely sexual one. This sign governs the feet, but it leads those born under it into clean, clear places, unless they themselves to its temptations and inherent weakness. These people are fond of responsibility, and usually be relied on to fill acceptably places es of trust. Those who bare to methodical business habits make excellent accountants, cashiers, and book-keepers. They are very few egotists to be found among Pisces people. In fact, they are in many instance abnormally deficient in self-esteem, and this causes them to appear very awkward, and sometimes leads to the belief that all the world is against them, and it is of no use try to keep up in the race with others, have a deep religious feeling, and because of their great persistence and natural loyalty, they cling to an early belief or a creed, even when they are very much shaken as to its correctness. When they do change they are apt to excuse themselves by saying it is not

THE INFLUENCE OF THE ZODIAC

so different after all from what they had previously believed. There is an innate modesty of both old and young born under this sign.

PERSONAL APPEARANCE

Pisces people are usually full faced, with placid, sleepy eyes, and apt to be round-shouldered.

COMPANIONS

They will find their most congenial friends and companions among Virgo and Capricorn people.

FAULTS

Worry, anxiety, and diseased imagination are the most formidable faults of this sign.

Some of these people heat their hearts out with imagining fears, and are constantly expecting accidents and unpleasant tidings. This anxiety makes them prematurely old. Many an active and earnest business man has taken his own life because of his gloomy forebodings of failure, and afterwards those fears were found to have been groundless. Pisces men, probably on account of their training and education, are more careful and methodical in their daily habits than Pisces women, although just as restless. The women are wavering and uncertain in all their actions. They lose their belongings, and mislay those of other people. They drop things and forget to pick them up, and sometimes are so superlatively careless in all household matters that even their sweet and helpful dispositions cannot make up for the trouble they create in a well-ordered household. These are the people who kick up mats and rugs, and never seem aware that they do not leave things exactly as they found them.

THE INFLUENCE OF THE ZODIAC

There is a peculiar obstinacy in the Pisces character, which sometimes becomes a most formidable element to deal with, and really seems inexplicable, but it is easily explained. The natural timidity and abnormal delicacy of these people acts as a constant restraint, and after a while the nature becomes tired of the yoke of its own placing and rebels. At this crisis they show a stubbornness which is even more disagreeable than that of the stiff-necked Taurus, and they have neither logic nor consistency. They will say and do the most absurd things, and stick to them. At such times, argument and advice are useless. The more they are reasoned with, the more obstinate they become. In the acceptance of a new theory or truth which they have previously repudiated, the males are quite likely to declare that it is precisely what they have always believed. One of the great faults of this sign is intellectual dishonesty.

Pisces people are apt to talk too much, and they have a tedious habit of asking questions. When united in marriage to those who object to giving an account of themselves, and who, as in the case of Libra people, have no patience with those who exact reasons and explanations, serious trouble in the inevitable result. Some of the people born under this sign are also very inattentive, and will interrupt a speaker or a conversation with the most irrelevant remarks, plainly showing that they have not understood a word that has been said. This causes them to appear very impolite, and sometimes exceedingly stupid. When told of their faults, their mortification leads them to a quick resentment or a deep-seated sullenness. Their faults can be summed up in restlessness, recklessness in giving, lack of judgment and discrimination, and disloyalty to self. These people are the ones who efface themselves for others, to the detriment of those they assist, and their own health and prosperity.

They are careless with their words, very illogical, constantly asking questions, and never waiting for answers.

THE INFLUENCE OF THE ZODIAC

DISEASES

The diseases to which Pisces people are subject are pains in the head, feet, and back, and weakness of the digestive organs. The male is often attacked by periods of despondency and self-censure, which lead to serious illness. The female is troubled by fits of melancholy and weeping, and frequently suffers from uterine difficulties. These ailments and every other known to man can he entirely dominated, forever cast out, by those who realize that mind is master and the body the servant of mind.

MODE OF GROWTH

People born under this sign should first of all learn the value of silence. They should have a private retiring place, a sanctuary, where for a few moments each day they can be safe from conflict and intrusion. They should not allow anything to break into these vitally necessary pauses. On such occasions they should hold every muscle and nerve in strict obedience to the will, compelling the body to absolute quiet. Their restlessness, anxiety, and heedlessness are at the bottom of much of the trouble that sometimes affects this peculiar but most lovable people. They must first learn to work out their own salvation before they accept the responsibility of saving others, and to realize that prodigality in giving always defeats the purpose of the giver. They should try to understand that money has made more vagabonds than poverty, and that the weakness of fond relatives has often driven to destruction those who might have been saved had they been wisely helped to self-reliance.

All those born under this sign should strive to develop their natural trust in an Infinite Power. This will prevent them from crossing bridges before they are built, and from the various apprehensions from which they constantly suffer. A good logos for them is "God understands," and still another more positive

THE INFLUENCE OF THE ZODIAC

one should be kept ever in mind. It is, "I can and I will, I can, and I will conquer my heedlessness, restlessness, my heart-breaking anxiety, the disposition to talk of myself, the foolish desire to help those whom God evidently intends shall help themselves. I can, and I will attend strictly to my own business. I can, and I will put a curb on all foolish emotions. I can, and I will hold my tongue; and I can, and I will become a willing and discreet server to humanity."

"I can, and I will," will be found an equally helpful and inspiring logos for every person who reads this book.

MARRIAGE

When a Pisces and a Virgo person are united in marriage, the offspring are usually very bright and intellectual. This is also true of a Pisces and Capricorn union, and the children are likely to be well formed and healthy in both cases, though there will be fewer offspring from the later union. Domestic comfort and satisfaction are the general results of such marriages. The domestic relations between Pisces and Gemini people are sometimes very harmonious, but Pisces and Libra people, and Pisces and Sagittarius people should not marry unless they have learned to conquer their faults. Those born under Libra are not happy in giving reasons, and those born under Sagittarius will give only such responses as suit themselves, and which are never satisfying to the Pisces mind.

GOVERNMENT OF CHILDREN

Many precocious little ones are born in this sign, and the average child is sensible, affable, kind-hearted, and exceedingly sensitive. Even in early childhood they do not like to be dependent upon others, and illustrate one of the chief weaknesses of the sign in the endeavor to give away all they possess. This trait, sweet and praiseworthy as it seems to the fond parent, is

THE INFLUENCE OF THE ZODIAC

one to be very carefully dealt with, as it frequently develops into dishonesty. If a Pisces child is not early restrained from and prodigality, he will deceive his guardians, and Sometimes take things that do not belong to him, to gratify this inordinate desire.

It is well to see that these children have a regular allowance, which is to cover certain clearly indicated expenses, as their future usefulness will he seriously impaired if they are not made to understand the value of money. They must be taught that an acknowledgment of their faults or their disobedience is something to be proud of, instead of something to be ashamed of. They should be treated with steady kindness, but they should be made feel the responsibility of their tasks and study.

Too much attention cannot be directed to the formation of neat and tidy habits, and a respect for other people's things. If they kick up a rug, they should be made to straighten it. If they lose or mislay their belongings, should be expected to find them without assialance, or to go without them. Every possible care should be given to development of the will power of these children. They sometimes show a peculiar obstinacy, which is mistaken for will, and which the parents foolishly talk of breaking. One might better break the neck of a Pisces child than attempt to break his will. His stubbornness is usually the result of shame, which owes its origin to real delicacy and sensitiveness, and which has been brought to the front by a mistake in government. These children should be led to think and to decide things for themselves by means of principles which they are exceedingly quick to understand if properly trained.

The governing planets are Jupiter and Neptune. The gems are chrysolite, pink-shell and moonstone. The astral colors are white, pink, emerald-green and black.

THE INFLUENCE OF THE ZODIAC

CHAPTER XX

An Explanation

In the application to our friends and acquaintances of the traits of character as expressed in the signs of the Zodiac, we shall occasionally be confronted with some one born perhaps squarely under a sign who does not appear to possess the qualities which belong to it. Perhaps the person will utterly disclaim the characteristics, especially the faults. This is not an uncommon occurrence, because the individual who is willing to admit his moral and spiritual overdoings and shortcomings is still rare enough to be called an anomaly. Sometimes, however, there is a real discrepancy between the alleged qualities and those possessed in reality. At such times it should be remembered that there are instances where some of the qualities of each sign in the triplicity seem to be represented by one person. One born under Taurus, for instance, may have some of the traits belonging to Virgo and Capricorn, and this is equally true of every triplicity. But the careful observer will soon find that the characteristics of the domains are unfailing.

There is as much difference, for example, between the people born in the domains of fire and water as there is between fire and water; as much difference between the people who come under the air and earth triplicities as between air and earth. A little study will make these facts plain to every investigator. When a planet or planets are strong at the time of birth, the characteristics of the signs are sometimes modified. Thus Saturn, being strong at the native's birth, may have much power over the Air Triplicity; Jupiter, being strong, would have the same effect upon the Fire Triplicity; Mars, being strong, would affect the Water Triplicity; Venus, being strong, would influence the Earth Triplicity. Then, again, those people who are brilliant in intellect and quick of impulse would be marked if the planet Uranus was

THE INFLUENCE OF THE ZODIAC

strong, as he governs the thinking and intellectual principle in man, being at home on his throne in Aquarius, which is the spiritual pole of the Air Triplicity; in fact, he exerts a marked influence upon all Air people. Again, Neptune, who is so little known, when powerful or in conjunction with powerful planets, wields a strong power over those horn under Aries and Pisces, the Head and Feet of the Grand Man. This planet governs the spiritual life and the invisible physiology of man, and is at home in either of these signs.

The ancient philosophers had seven planets and the Zodiac upon which to base their calculations, Uranus and Neptune being unknown. Their judgment of character by these signs was phenomenally correct. "Everything else in the universe may lie," those wise men used to say, "but the Zodiac always tells the truth."

THE INFLUENCE OF THE ZODIAC

IN CLOSING

"If ye he led by the Spirit, ye are not under the Law. "

It is the purpose of this book to teach that spirit is absolute, and that solar and planetary action can have no power over the spiritual man. "He is born a natural body, he is raised a spiritual body"- not after death, but NOW. When he finds his center, establishes his Tri-unity, he is Monarch of himself and King of Circumstance. The man who does not advance loses ground. He who has not the spirit of his age will be crushed under the misery of it. He who remains ignorant of his genius or talent will be blown about by every breeze of opinion and every wind of doctrine. The definition of ignorance is sin, sickness, sorrow, and death.

The progressive student will soon find that his power depends upon the harmonious development of his natural genius, and the establishment of true polarity. He will live each day a willing server, his mind ever fixed on the boundless opulence of nature, able to look steadfastly through nature up to nature's God.

THE END

Printed in Great Britain
by Amazon